Effective HR Management in the Union Environment

A CLV Special Report

Jamie Knight

CARSWELL
A THOMSON COMPANY

National Library of Canada Cataloguing in Publication

Knight, Jamie
    Effective HR management in the union environment / Jamie Knight.

(A CLV special report)
ISBN 0-459-27732-4

    1. Personnel management. 2. Open and closed shop. 3. Labor laws and legislation—Ontario. I. Title. II. Series: CLV special report series

HD8106.K55 2002   658.3   C2002-903933-9

CARSWELL

A THOMSON COMPANY

One Corporate Plaza, 2075 Kennedy Road, Toronto, Ontario M1T 3V4
Customer Relations:
Toronto 1-416-609-3800
Elsewhere in Canada/U.S. 1-800-387-5162
Fax 1-416-298-5094

Brief Contents

Contents

CONTENTS

CONTENTS

Acknowledgments

This book is a companion to a book entitled, "Managing Your Union-Free Workplace". To a large extent, much of what you read in this book also appears in "Union-Free". That is because of my central position that management should try to operate its workplaces in a way that suits management, whether or not you have to deal with a union. Even so, there are obvious differences. Effective HR Management in the Union Environment is written as a guide for the management of human resources in a unionized workplace. As such, although much is the same as "Union-Free", there is also much that has significantly changed. My acknowledgments are essentially the same for both books, as my influences are consistent for whatever workplace requests my advice and assistance.

Good human resources management is built on personal relationships. To be effective, you should be interested in people – all sorts of people. You should like people. You should expect a great deal from people and from yourself. When your expectations are met, you should celebrate, then expect even more. In this way, effective human resources management also builds personal relationships.

As a professional working in human resources, I have a strong belief that people are special. Each person is unique. Certainly, there are standards to set and procedures to follow, but there are no cookie cutters. Every day is full of new challenges. Every person with whom we work has the potential to wow us and test us in new and marvellous ways, or at least ways that cause us to marvel. No solution that we achieve today will govern all of our tomorrows.

Personal relationships are both the root and the flower of good human resources management. With that in mind, I want to open this book with some comments about my background, my career and some important people whom I have met along the way. I trust that they will help to illustrate some of the points that will be made throughout the book.

I went to law school without much idea of what would happen afterwards. After two years of under-achievement, I took a year off and went to Europe with my girlfriend. Betty was still my girlfriend when we returned seven months later, so we got married. It was five months before law school started again and I needed a job. By blind luck, I was available about a month ahead of the other university students, who were still in the midst of writing exams. I was hired by what was then called the Toronto General Hospital. Essentially my job was to hire the other university students to summer positions as soon as their exams ended. That is how I started my career in human resources. It was 1981.

There is no substitute for luck, and mine was to continue. I secured an articling position with one of the premier boutique labour law firms in Ontario, Mathews, Dinsdale & Clark. I am no longer there, but the firm's high reputation has been unscarred by my early departure. In between articles and working as an associate with MDC, I worked for a couple of years in-house with Versa Services, now known as Aramark Canada. As a young labour lawyer, Versa was a terrific place to start. They had food service and cleaning contracts all over the place, all across Canada. I was always negotiating collective agreements or acting in arbitration cases, and Versa dealt with just about every union you could think of. In the process, I got to discover Canada and very small planes.

Since 1988, I have benefitted from the wisdom and support of my colleagues in the law firm once known as Fraser & Beatty, now called Fraser Milner Casgrain LLP. FMC is a leading National Business Law firm, with a wonderful group of employment and labour lawyers, not only in Toronto, but also in five other offices, from Montreal to Vancouver. At present, we have 15 labour and employment lawyers in Toronto and some 40 labour and employment lawyers in our offices across Canada.

I have met some fine people in my 20 years in human resources – including lawyers, arbitrators, managers, employees, public servants and union representatives. It is always risky to name names, because there are always others who could have been named and I will apologize in advance to those I leave out. That said, there are seven people whom I have singled out for special mention. I hope they won't mind.

First, I want to acknowledge my parents, Ed and Margie Knight. They are now both retired, although thankfully healthy and very active. My father was a school principal for many years. What impressed me most was how much Dad was admired and appreciated by his staff. He challenged his people to achieve excellence and to pursue the objectives of their profession, which was to teach their brains out and to open up the world to the students with whom they had been entrusted. The teachers who worked for my Dad were all union members. They were also dedicated professionals.

My mother taught me her own lesson, from which all of us can learn. After choosing to devote many years to raising four children, Mom went back to school, completed her degree and became qualified in the very specialized area of teaching children with learning disabilities. Living in Canada in the 21st century, most of us are blessed with good health and long careers. It is never too late to take on new challenges and to excel in areas that are of great importance to the communities in which we live.

At Versa Services, I had a boss who was larger than life, a real character. Some of you reading this may know Phil Coupey. I had more good luck – I got to work for Phil before I knew much of anything. Phil taught me two of the most valuable lessons that I have learned. The first lesson occurred in my first week of work. We had a grievance to deal with in one of our locations. Who can remember what it was about, it doesn't matter. What matters is that I researched the heck out of this problem and very proudly showed up in Phil's office with a ten-page memorandum, including footnotes. Phil threw it in the garbage and said something like this: "First, I only read one page, maybe two if I am really interested. Second, I know that you went to law school, you don't have to prove it to me, just tell me what you think we should do."

The second lesson happened during my first set of collective agreement negotiations. I had all of my creative engines firing. In those days, we did not have laptops to tap away at, but I madly scribbled proposals, counter-proposals, packages and alternatives on mounds of paper. I worked well into the wee hours of the morning and came out with a collective agreement that everyone thought was a pretty good resolution. Phil had come to watch me in action, but he went to bed at 10 p.m. The next day, when we were driving back to Toronto, with me crashed in the back seat, Phil asked me how I thought I had done. I said that I was pretty pleased with myself. Phil said that I worked too hard.

When you are involved in human resources, you should be patient. As a patient person, let other people do some of the work. This includes union representatives. Open up participation in the evolution of the ideas that eventually become resolutions. You cannot solve all of the problems all by yourself, even though you may be technically capable and sufficiently energetic to do just that. If you work too hard and if you try too hard to drag people kicking and screaming to a settlement, then your solution may have no more strength than the paper upon which it is written.

The fourth person is my law partner and good friend, Kristin Taylor. Kristin sometimes claims that I have taught her a few things along the way, but I have probably learned much more than I have taught. There are three lessons that Kristin has taught particularly well. The first is that employment lawyers — and all Human Resources Professionals ("HRP's") — are in a service business. The best advice in the world may be of little use unless it is also prompt. The second lesson is that there is no substitute for excellence. HRP's and employment lawyers are dealing with the most precious asset of any organization – people. In helping to create the finest workplaces we can and in maximizing the productivity of the workplaces for which we are responsible, we should strive to be excellent in our work and we should demand excellence in others. The third lesson is that people really matter. Everyone has the potential to contribute. Some have more potential than others and some use more of the potential that they have. Great results can come from the most unexpected places. Kristin never gives up on anyone until that person gives up. At some point an employment relationship has to end, but we often rush to that point with reckless energy, when we should be spending our time and efforts in helping someone find and use the potential that s/he has.

The fifth person on my list is no longer with us, but he remains a big part of me. Brent Snell was killed suddenly in June 2000. He was 42 and full of life. Brent was widely admired, and the many persons who knew him, even people who did not know him very well, have keenly felt his loss. Of his many attributes, there are two features of Brent that continue to guide me. First, he had a very good sense of what was right and he did not allow himself to be pulled off line when travelling the right course. Second, he listened very carefully to other people, so that they felt valuable and they felt that Brent valued them. Brent did not do this in any calculated manner; he was genuinely interested in all kinds of other people, most especially if they were very different from him. The effect was profound – people who are listened to, who feel valuable and who feel that another person values them are incredibly loyal to that person. Without even trying, Brent commanded great loyalty from a wide and varied group of people.

The sixth person is my close friend, Ron Charbon. As far as I can tell, Ron is convinced that every problem can be solved with determination and good cheer. If the problem seems too big, Ron simply breaks it up into smaller problems, then solves those.

The seventh and final person I want to mention is the most pleasant person I know, my wife Betty. Everything that you need to know about dealing with other people you can learn from Betty. She is quick to praise good efforts, knowing that the results will follow. She does not hesitate to point out laziness and carelessness, knowing that the individual person is not fundamentally flawed. Most lazy and careless people have yet to meet the acceptable standard (whether it is picking up discarded clothes or writing an essay on folk heroes in children's literature). That is what managers and leaders are for, to set high standards and insist that the standards are met. Most of all, Betty takes great joy in all aspects of life; she recognizes that it is all an adventure. Open your eyes and see opportunity, even in the smallest actions. It is easy to find fault in each other, but there is so much more in each of us to appreciate and admire. It is from Betty that I have learned to look past the flaws that all of us have and focus instead on the virtues that are there to be found. Each member of your workplace can make positive contributions or they would not have been hired in the first place. A little effort and the right attitude may be all that is needed to bring positive contributions to the surface.

The observations and recommendations in the pages that follow come from twenty years of experience in human resources and in the practice of labour and employment law. I have been fortunate to teach with the University of Guelph, Office of Open Learning for the past twelve years. I have been involved with two recurring courses in particular: Labour and Employment Law, which is a course sanctioned by the Human Resources Professionals Association of Ontario and part of the CHRP program. The other course is a Supervisory Development Program that focuses on teaching front-line and second-line supervisors, the essentials of management, including the legal aspects of human resources management. Many of the ideas in these pages come from those two courses and the enthusiastic participants I have met.

Many of the other ideas come from my partners and colleagues at my law firm, Fraser Milner Casgrain LLP, as well as my professional colleagues who specialize in labour and employment law, whether acting for employers, unions or individual employees. I have enjoyed the confidence of executives, managers and human resources professionals for a wide variety of clients over the years, as well as the union representatives who have sat on the other side of the table. To all of them, and to all of you, I extend my thanks.

Finally, I would like to express my appreciation and thanks to Derry McDonell of Carswell, who encouraged me to organize my thoughts in this book, and who remained patient while I did so.

In the usual way, although I have had many sources for ideas, any errors or instances of clumsy drafting are entirely my responsibility. I may well be asked to improve on my work in the future. Please feel free to send me your own thoughts, criticisms or examples. My e-mail address is jamie.knight@fmc-law.com. I cannot promise a response, but I can promise my interest in your views.

Jamie Knight
Port Credit, Ontario, May 2002

◆
INTRODUCTION

Good human resource management is an important key to the success of Canadian workplaces. It is an inescapable requirement in workplaces that have unionized employees. In general terms, the objective of good human resources management is to achieve a balance as you strive to understand and meet the needs and goals of the different players in the workplace. A unionized workplace requires you to try to achieve and maintain a three-way balance between the personal aspirations and idiosyncrasies of the employees, the objectives of the trade union that represents them, and the overall purpose for the organization, be it primarily motivated by profit (private sector) or service (public sector).

In very specific terms, a key objective of good human resources management in a unionized workplace is to minimize the impact of the union on the employer's ability to achieve organizational objectives. For most employers, recognizing the needs of the employees on the one hand and being a champion for the objectives of the employer on the other hand, while trying to keep the union from tilting the balance, most successfully achieves the general human resources objective, of creating and maintaining a balanced workplace. The best chance that an organization has of minimizing the involvement of the union in the workplace is found in the pursuit of excellent human resources management.

Ignore the Union

In the pages that follow, a major theme is that unionized workplaces can improve their human resources management by forgetting about the fact that they have to deal with a union. This suggestion is neither meant to demean unions, nor is it meant to create false expectations. What I mean is that management should stop using the union as an excuse for poor communications with the employees, poor productivity and the absence of common objectives. To the extent possible, and always in a manner consistent with the requirements of the collective agreement and the law, management should try to manage the workplace without allowing the union to push them off course.

Unions exist to represent the interests of their members, who are the "rank and file" employees. This does not have to mean that unions exist to oppose the interests of the employer. Indeed, in the present-day economy, it is increasingly apparent to many employers and unions that there is considerable overlap between the best interests of the employer and the best interests of the employees who are union members. This may be especially true in respect of Canadian companies that are part of large North American or international organizations.

In managing human resources, with the objective of ignoring the union, unionized workplaces should focus on many of the same principles that I would recommend for non-union workplaces. Of course, you cannot simply pretend that the collective agreement does not exist. On the other hand, employers should not allow the collective agreement to subvert the special character of the workplace or to obliterate its unique history and culture. In particular, employers should keep the focus on pursuing legitimate management objectives. Employers should strive to avoid negotiating collective agreement provisions that are inconsistent with those objectives. Similarly, employers should not allow themselves to interpret or apply the collective agreement in a manner that is contrary to those objectives.

It should be pointed out that unionized workplaces could have some unexpected advantages for employers. These advantages are derived from the fact that the negotiation and administration of a collective agreement has the inevitable impact of improving the human resources structure, or at least making it more evident. This structure includes the legal requirement for a formal complaints procedure, complete with third party resolution (the grievance and arbitration process), which provides an outlet for employee unhappiness. Non-union employers are rightly content with the freedom that comes from not having to deal with a trade union. On the other hand, unionized employers are often pleasantly surprised at the efficiency and self-discipline that comes with having to manage under the restrictions of a collective agreement.

I am not expecting unionized employers to give thanks for their collective agreements. Indeed, my main point is to encourage unionized workplaces to manage the workplace the way they want, without being unduly hemmed in by the union or the collective agreement. I am simply pointing out that many union workplaces provide a structure that is useful, both in general and in respect of many of the component parts. At the very least, this structure should be understood. As a unionized workplace builds its framework of good human resources management, the framework that is required because of the collective agreement and applicable laws can provide a very helpful starting point. Just remember that it is only a start. Union or non-union, management is responsible for the operation of the workplace.

I should be clear from the outset that it is not the intention of this book to focus on tactics that you could use to create a climate that would encourage employees to terminate the bargaining rights of their union. The rules of union decertification are quite particular and differ in each of the provincial jurisdictions and in the federal jurisdiction. It is very unlikely that you would be able to "ignore the union" to the point of getting rid of them. If that happens in your workplace, you may be very pleased with the result. For most unionized workplaces, decertification is a pipedream and can be a very unhealthy waste of your time and energy.

Instead, I am interested in providing you with ideas that will help to establish a framework for managing your human resources in a relatively stable workplace environment that is unionized and will likely remain so for the indefinite future. In this respect, I am working from a foundation that is based on three assumptions:

- if you are using this book, you are probably working in a unionized workplace;
- if you are a member of management or a human resources professional ("HRP") in a unionized workplace, then you probably expect that your workplace will continue to be unionized and it is probably a significant part of your job to help manage human resources within the unionized framework; and
- it is undoubtedly also your goal and part of your job to operate the best workplace possible and to manage your human resources in a manner that helps them achieve their very best in conjunction with operational objectives.

Mixed Workplaces

Many employers have workplaces in which some subordinate employees are in one or more bargaining units, while other subordinate employees are non-union. I maintain the view that ignoring the union and focusing on management's objectives is important. That said, the partially unionized employer should pay close attention to the terms and conditions of the collective agreement and the overall nature of the relationship with the union in order to avoid creating an incentive for the non-union employees to select a union representative.

This is, in effect, a very particular variation of the theme that permeates my book, *"Union-Free"*. In that book, I argue that non-union workplaces have much to learn from unionized workplaces. In mixed workplaces, it is inevitable that the non-union part of the workplace will have much that must be applied based on what is happening with the unionized workers. It has to work this way because the employer has no choice but to bargain with the union and make reasonable efforts to achieve a collective agreement. Once achieved, the collective agreement and the application of the agreement define the unionized framework. It is generally desirable to have consistency throughout the workplace. The best way to achieve consistency, and to manage the workplace without an artificial barrier between union members and other employees, is to apply much of the unionized framework across the entire workplace.

Indeed, it should be noted that every workplace that has unionized employees is, to some degree, mixed. There are always management employees and others who cannot become unionized. While there may be some differences in how these different employees are treated, much of the framework should be consistent throughout the workplace, including management. Again, because the existence of a union necessarily establishes significant elements of the framework, the overall framework to apply will be, to a large extent, derived from the relationship with the trade union.

The Importance of Good Human Resources Management

If the processes of employee relations are conducted effectively, the following results should be expected:

- management will be informed and knowledgeable, and committed to continuation of effective labour relations processes;
- plans to make changes in programs, technology, policies and procedures will take into consideration the perspectives of the employees and their union representatives;
- operational objectives will be achieved with minimal conflict; people will work together on issues, as will the employer and the union; operations will be efficient and effective in pursuit of objectives and in resolving issues;
- the different elements of the collective agreement and the human resources framework will be applied consistently and fairly;
- any complaint or suggestion and any grievance will get a timely and effective response;
- employee morale will be high, which not only is more pleasant for everyone, but also fosters enhanced productivity;
- there will be fewer requests for clarification of straightforward policies or terms and conditions of employment; and
- there will be fewer situations that require the third part intervention of an arbitrator or of the labour board.

If, on the other hand, the processes of employee relations are ineffective, management may be exposed to the following risks:

- loss of productivity and service;
- inconsistent application of policies or terms of the collective agreement or elements of the human resources framework, resulting in low morale and increased costs;
- many complaints and grievances, and few positive suggestions;
- escalation of conflict, which increases the risk of litigation, either at arbitration or at the labour board;
- too much management time spent dealing with employee relations and union issues at the expense of program issues;
- reactive and crisis-oriented relationships;
- over-reliance on third-party participation (public servants, arbitrators and labour boards) to achieve the resolution of disputes.

Management must focus continuously on employee relations to ensure that employees work effectively and efficiently for the benefit of the organization. You should strive to manage all aspects of employee relations in a consistent and objective manner. Effective management will foster enhanced productivity, expeditious dispute resolution, good morale, and efficient communications. Achieving these objectives will depend upon the effective co-ordination of the interests of the workplace parties. With sensitivity, leadership and planning, these different interests can be satisfied with minimal conflict.

◆

CHAPTER 1

THE WORKPLACE PLAYERS

I n a unionized workplace, the parties include workers, one or more unions, inside and outside union representatives, supervisors, higher-level management, professionals, confidential staff and third parties who are typically present in the workplace. From a human resources standpoint, all of these players are necessary and must be suitably managed, directed, or at least acknowledged in order to carry out the objectives of the organization in an effective and efficient manner.

Before proceeding further, we should take a closer look at the players in the workplace.

Workers

In law, all sorts of people are employees, from casual workers right up to the president, who may also be the owner and majority shareholder. For our purposes, the term "workers" will be used to refer to subordinate employees, the so-called rank and file, who carry out instructions, but who do not typically instruct or direct other workers. These subordinate employees are the members or potential members of bargaining units represented by trade unions.

In a manufacturing plant, workers fall into two main groups, white-collar or blue-collar. Most unionized plants have at least a blue-collar unit. Some have both. It is rare, but possible, to have a white-collar unit without a blue-collar unit. In almost every case, blue-collar is separate from white-collar for purposes of union organization, although the same union may represent both groups.

Workers in shipping and receiving, as well as drivers, are typically grouped with the blue-collar workers, while sales are grouped with the white collars. Laboratory, quality control, and technical staff may be blue or white depending on the precise nature and location of their work. For the purposes of bargaining units, workers include lead hands or group leaders and sometimes even working managers, depending on how much authority is actually given to such leading employees.

In an office setting, workers are typically all in one employee group, no matter how many different classifications there may be. In certain specialized sectors, like health care, workers may be considered to be in different groupings, depending on the nature of their work. For example, nurses are grouped separately from other workers, sometimes even when those other workers have extensive overlap with nurses in terms of the jobs actually performed.

Workers can be part-time or full-time, regularly scheduled or on call. They can be short-term employees or "lifers". Student employees are workers. Workers can have specific contracts of employment, written or oral, with or without a defined duration, or they can simply be employed on a handshake or a nod. Some workers will have been around so long, that nobody can remember the terms and conditions of hire, if there were any.

To the surprise of many organizations, workers may also include contract personnel or even agency workers. It is one thing to bring in an agency employee for a few days or even a few weeks. It can become quite another thing when the agency employee stays around for several weeks or even months, even if on a part-time and casual basis. The employment relationship is not determined by who is signing the wage cheques. What is fundamental to the determination is who is in control. The party in control is typically the party that schedules and directly supervises the work. After the first couple of weeks (if not the first couple of hours), it is usually the party that is in control of where the work is being performed that is in control of the worker.

Lead Hands or Group Leaders

Especially in a production plant, it is common to have certain workers used as leaders of a work group, line or shift. These workers, who often have a special level of experience or expertise, fall below the level of supervisor, because they do not perform traditional management functions, as will be discussed immediately below. For the most part, they co-ordinate the flow of work, help to schedule production, and are instrumental in on-the-job-training. It is typical for lead hands to have a wide knowledge of many jobs in the plant, so they can fill in, either to replace missing workers, or as may be required to fulfill the needs of production. In a shift operation, especially in a smaller plant, lead hands may be the most senior employee on site during night and weekend shifts. In such cases, the lead hand would be considered to be a supervisor for the purposes of health and safety legislation, and would naturally take on many supervisory duties for the purposes of performance management.

Notwithstanding the close relationship between lead hands and management, lead hands are generally on the other side of the line and would be included in a typical blue-collar bargaining unit. Depending on the extent of their authority, some office managers or supervisors may actually have a lead hand kind of role in a white-collar unit and, therefore, be part of the bargaining unit.

Skilled Employees and Professional Workers

Skilled employees, such as electricians, millwrights, tool and die makers and licensed mechanics, are typically included in the blue-collar bargaining unit in a manufacturing plant. Other non-managerial employees are less likely to fit easily with either the blue-collar or white-collar group of workers. They will be either in between, in something of a grey zone, or more clearly separate. These professional workers include quality specialists, laboratory technicians, engineers and computer programmers and technicians.

Depending on the nature of the service business or office environment, there also may be distinct groupings of professionals in a non-manufacturing setting. These employees are not managers, but they have unique and advanced skills that separate them from other white-collar workers.

Bargaining Units

It is important to be clear about this term, which has been used a number of times already in this book. For the most part, Canadian jurisdictions require unions to organize groups of employees who are all employed by a single employer. As stated above, there could be more than one bargaining unit within each employer. If there are different bargaining units, they could be represented by the same union or different unions. Even if it is the same union, there could be different locals. If the employer has multiple locations, they could be unionized separately. Indeed, many employers will have different employee groups in different locations performing similar functions — some of them will be unionized and others will be non-union. If there are multiple locations within a geographical area (such as a municipality or county), the locations could be unionized separately or there could be a regional bargaining unit.

Front-Line Supervisors

Front-line supervisors have a job that is both difficult and vitally important for successful human resources management. An employee does not become a supervisor, as a matter of law, just because s/he has that title or because s/he gets a salary instead of an hourly wage. The determining factor is whether or not the employee has economic power over other employees. The most obvious indication of economic power is the authority of the supervisor to hire and fire employees. A person who, acting alone, cannot hire or fire will still be considered a supervisor if his or her recommendation carries significant weight with the ultimate decision-maker. Understand that the mere ability to make a recommendation is not sufficient. To be a supervisor, and therefore part of management, the recommendation must be an effective one. It may not always carry the day, but generally it will receive careful consideration by the ultimate decision-maker.

Another aspect of economic power that would indicate supervisory status is the responsibility to discipline, especially if discipline could involve unpaid time off, even if that is as basic as having the power to send an employee home in the middle of the shift. As well, a supervisor typically would make or participate in decisions about promotions, demotions, lay-offs and significant work assignments. A supervisor also would be able to grant paid time off, whether prior to the end of a shift or scheduling vacation or lieu time.

For the most part, and in most Canadian jurisdictions, a supervisor cannot be part of a bargaining unit and is not entitled to union representation. Even if there is a supervisory bargaining unit, it is typically separate and distinct from the workers.

The importance of the front-line supervisor to the management of human resources in most workplaces is that s/he is the one who is most directly responsible for ensuring the efficient and effective operation of the workplace on a day-to-day basis. The supervisor may have some hand in the formation of policies, procedures and rules. Through day-to-day practices, the front-line supervisor is sure to be much more prominent in the implementation and, especially, the ongoing application of policy. The supervisor is typically the member of management who has first-hand or, at least, the best second-hand information about key incidents that occur in the workplace. In any situations involving issues of fundamental policy, discipline, safety or human rights, it is usually the supervisor who will be the key witness for management.

The front-line supervisor is also the member of the management team who is closest to the non-managerial employees. In many cases, the supervisor will have been promoted from "the ranks" and will still be plugged into the network that was built up while s/he was one of the workers. Even if hired from outside the workplace, a supervisor will often have values and experiences that are much closer to the workers than other members of the management team. It is quite natural that the supervisor will feel the pull of conflicting loyalties. While this sometimes can be a frustration to more senior levels of management, it is very helpful in any situation of crisis, such as a union organizing campaign or a potential work stoppage (strike or lockout). It is fundamental to the successful operation of any workplace, especially one in crisis, to be able to rely on the two-way communication stream that is created by a trusted and accessible supervisor.

In a unionized workplace, the front-line supervisor has direct responsibility for the application of the collective agreement. It is the responsibility of the supervisor to ensure that employees are entitled to the rights that have been negotiated between the union and the employer. The supervisor also has direct responsibility for the imposition of discipline or, at least, to initiate the disciplinary process through the identification and initial investigation of incidents of misconduct.

Given that the supervisor is such a key contact point between management and the workers, and given the important day-to-day responsibilities of supervisors, it is very important for all organizations to invest time in and pay attention to the selection, training, and ongoing support of the front-line supervisors. Of all the lessons in human resources management that could be taught to the senior members of the management team, the two most important concern the supervisors. These lessons are two sides of the same coin:

1. Trust your supervisors, and provide them with the training and the tools necessary to administer the collective agreement, to exercise discretion when required, to support and enforce workplace

standards, and to take effective action in support of the objectives of the management team.

2. Although the decisions of a front-line supervisor should not be supported at all costs, the supervisor should be supported at all times. If senior management has problems with the performance of a supervisor, it should deal with those problems in confidence and without creating a scapegoat for disaffected workers. You should be vigilant at all times not to cut your supervisor off at the knees. A front-line supervisor's authority must be built up, layer by layer. Unsupportive decisions of senior management that rashly interfere with supervisory actions can slice through the authority of a supervisor in a moment, thereby creating significant and sometimes irreparable harm. The harm created is to the very person who you need to rely on to run part or all of the workplace on a day-to-day basis. Undercut your front-line supervisors, and you are undercutting all of management.

Higher Level Management

Even in organizations with very flat management structures, it is generally the case that you will have second and higher tiers of management. These people may be very involved with the workers and they may be in direct and frequent communication with them; however, they remain at least one step removed in terms of hierarchy, such that the day-to-day supervision of the work force is, or ought to be, directed through a front-line supervisor.

A challenge for higher-level management is to create direct and meaningful bonds with the workers while, at the same time, respecting and reinforcing the primary human resources responsibilities of the supervisor. It is important that higher level management does not create an informal hierarchy that essentially serves to bypass the formal hierarchy, such that the decisions of a supervisor, at least in important situations, become easily revised or even contradicted.

In a unionized workplace, higher-level management will become directly involved with the trade union in two different ways:

1. At the later stages of the grievance procedure; and
2. In collective bargaining.

In both situations, it is important that higher-level management not become a separate and distinct voice of management. Management should act as a team. There should be consistency and continuity in the decision-making process. In a grievance situation, the later stages of the grievance procedure provide an opportunity for further reflection and, possibly, for reasonable compromise. In collective bargaining, the management negotiating team should be fully informed about the concerns of the front-line supervisor and careful not to betray those concerns or fall into the easy trap of using the supervisors as scapegoats when there are disputes about management practices in the workplace. Indeed, it is important that management proposals properly reflect the real issues of the front-line supervisors, so that they can be supported by the decisions that the management negotiating team makes at the table. It is fundamentally important to understand that the restrictions created by the language of the collective agreement will have a significant and far-reaching impact on supervisors in their pursuit of management objectives as they manage their subordinate workers on a day-to-day basis.

Human Resources Professionals ("HRP's") and other Professional Staff

There is an important decision that organizations should make about the role of HRP's in human resources management. This should not be an accidental decision, but a deliberate choice. Is human resources management to be the responsibility of your operational supervisors and managers, or is it the responsibility of the HRP's? In my view, there is only one good choice. Operational management has to be responsible to manage its own people. The role of HRP's is still very significant, but it is a role of support and guidance. Everything that is written in this book is based on this fundamental design of human resources management: the people who are ultimately responsible for the quality and quantity of the goods and services must manage the people who are producing the goods or providing the services.

It is for this reason that the operations management should be directly involved in policy development, even if that effort is co-ordinated and led by HRP's. Operations management must also be involved in a decisive role in such key human resources situations as hiring, promotions, staffing levels, performance appraisals, discipline and dismissals.

When you gather your management team together and ask the question, "who among you are human resources professionals", you want every hand to be raised.

There are other professionals who will likely have a significant support role to play in human resources management even if they do not have direct supervisory authority. These professionals include those on the financial side of the organization — internal auditors, accountants, and controllers — as well as those on the mechanical and engineering side. Some organizations will also have internal legal staff members who may be very helpful in reviewing policies and any draft language that is used in collective agreements, settlements and correspondence, even if they are not expert in labour and employment law.

The keys for all who manage or support human resources, and for HRP's in particular, are, first to know the objectives of your organization, then try to bring out the full potential of all the people with whom you work within the organization in ways that will maximize the achievement of the objectives.

Confidential Staff

In all workplaces there are likely to be non-managerial clerical or secretarial workers who have a separate and unique status by virtue of who directs their work and the nature of the work that they perform. Confidential staff members have normal access to personnel records and to key information about the business. Typically, confidential staff members work in the human resources area or for company executives or the senior management of a plant or office. For the most part, confidential staff will be excluded from bargaining units.

Third Parties

Many workplaces have third parties who are routinely on site, either on an indefinite basis, or for limited terms. In this respect, I do not include agency workers, who are essentially doing the same kind of work as workers who are directly employed, and who may be or become employees as a matter of law. Rather, my reference is to third parties who have distinct roles to play in respect of the peripheral functions of the workplace. They may be cleaners, security staff, or food service employees. They may be involved in construction, maintenance, equipment installation, data processing or temporary situations involving the implementation of technological change. They may even be involved at higher levels of management, including such people as accountants, outside auditors, consultants, benefits brokers, pension fund managers, and lawyers who specialize in such areas of the law as employment, labour, human rights, health and safety, and pensions and benefits.

We usually think of third parties in terms of other companies. In a company with multiple plants and offices, third parties may also be workers, professionals or managerial employees from other plants or offices.

Many modern workplaces have taken to contracting out peripheral functions. As well, specialized short-term projects often will be carried out by teams of outside contractors or specialized teams that move from plant to plant or from office to office within a larger organization.

Employee Organizations and Representatives

The most obvious employee organization is the trade union itself. In addition to the trade union, it is important for management to understand, promote and co-operate with the formal and less formal employee organizations that are active in the workplace.

The organization that is most like a trade union is an employee association, which in its most formal state may negotiate something that legally is, or is very like, a collective agreement. An employee association may also represent employees in individual disputes with the employer.

If an employee association truly represents the workers and is formally recognized by the employer, and if it negotiates terms and conditions of employment in an agreement that is legally ratified or approved by the workers who are represented by the association, then the employer may be able to avoid union organizing activity except during the limited open periods that are provided for in labour legislation. These open periods occur during the last few months of the term of the agreement. If the legal requirements were met, the employee association would have the same legal status as a trade union. Legal status does not require that the employee association be affiliated with any pre-existing trade union or labour organization.

As a very important note of caution, employers are not supposed to be involved in the creation, administration or ongoing support of an employee association. If the employees are not able to establish and maintain an association on their own, then the workplace will remain completely vulnerable to union organizing activity.

It should be pointed out that some employers have had excellent success with employee associations. Other employers have found, over time, that an employee association is not only on a legal par with a trade union, but it is for practical purposes the same thing. In other words, some employee associations can be as difficult for an employer to deal with as a regular trade union.

There may be other employee organizations in a workplace that primarily exist for a social or benevolent purpose. Even though these groups may be informal and may not have any involvement with the terms and conditions of employment, by their mere existence and operation they can still provide some degree of leadership and common purpose to a group of employees, separate and apart from the union or association.

There are also employee representatives who naturally evolve or who are required by law or the collective agreement in all but the smallest workplaces, at least for the purposes of health and safety, but often for other policy purposes as well. These representatives are typically elected or appointed by employees under the supervision of the trade union. In some cases, groups will include representatives of different trade unions that are active in the workplace as well as non-union employees. These mixed committees or work groups will often have their own unique dynamic, which can flourish separate and apart from any of the substantive issues that may be dealt with. Management should encourage the positive development of such groups and should maintain contact, but not expect to control them.

Any time that input would be useful, from policy formation to work methods, management should reach out to include worker representatives. This will not only enrich decision-making, but will also create natural bonds that may become useful in pursuing the objectives of the workplace as distinct from the objectives of the union. In this respect, remember my earlier premise, that management in a unionized workplace should ignore the union and continue to focus on achieving legitimate management objectives. Do not allow yourself to be thrown off course by the presence of the union.

◆

CHAPTER 2

THE BOUNDARIES OF HUMAN RESOURCES MANAGEMENT

This book favours a practical approach to human resources management; however, good practices should be built on sound theory. It is important to understand key legal concepts that impact on human resources management.

In my experience, even without a good knowledge of the law, you probably will find that you are managing your human resources in a lawful manner so long as you engage in common sense management. Both common sense and the law require that your human resources decisions be exercised in good faith, and with the kind of respect and concern for your people that you would expect in an advanced democracy like Canada.

In this section, we will review the central concept of management rights. We will then examine the boundaries that restrict management in its operation of the workplace. In particular, we will review the boundaries created by centuries of common law, made by judges, and decades of statutory law, made by elected politicians and their legislative assemblies, as well as the boundaries created by the collective agreement.

In addition to the strict legal boundaries within which employers must operate, there are certain other boundaries that impact on how people are managed in Canadian workplaces. To a very real degree, these additional boundaries are self-imposed. That is, they represent limitations that management quite properly imposes on itself, especially if it is acting knowledgeably and in a responsible manner.

The fundamental starting place is that management can do whatever it wants in pursuit of the objectives of the workplace, subject to the restrictive boundaries. In other words, management does not have to look for permission to do whatever it wants. Instead, management has to look to see if it is restricted or prevented from doing what it wants. If one or more of the boundaries that we will review shortly does not limit it, then management is free to act as it sees fit.

To put this in a visual context, imagine that you are constructing a one-room building in an open field. You start with the field, stretching out as far as you can see in every direction. That is management in its original state, free to do whatever it wants — what it thinks is necessary to achieve the business or institutional objectives. As we will soon see, this is not a normal building. The boundaries that we are forced to put up in a couple of cases and that we choose to put up in a couple of other cases are not solid, or at least not throughout. There are wide-open spaces in each of the boundaries that maintain considerable freedom for management. The open field remains, but not in all places and not for all purposes.

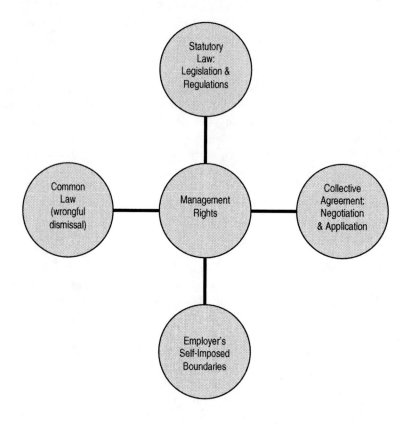

There are four walls or four boundaries on management rights. Not only are the walls not solid throughout, but also these boundaries are not entirely fixed. Indeed, all of the boundaries are subject to some adjustment through the intervention of management, even though they all remain to some degree as limitations on management's freedom to act. The preceeding diagram shows the boundaries that limit the exercise of management rights.

As we proceed to construct the four walls of our building, the task for those of you involved in human resources management will be to find ways to achieve what you need to do within the building itself or to try to modify the limitations created by each boundary so that you can stretch beyond the boundaries. You can only learn to live within the walls or to transform the walls if you achieve an initial understanding of the boundaries themselves. Please note that, at this point, we will only seek to introduce concepts. Some of the key concepts will be explored more fully in later chapters.

The First Boundary — The Common Law

The first boundary is the common law. The common law is what is sometimes referred to as judge-made law. In Canada, the common law is derived from our British heritage, and comes to us after almost ten centuries of adjudicating individual disputes. In particular, the common law has taken shape since the invention of the printing press at the end of the 15th century. With increasing ease, the ability to copy text automatically has allowed for the recording and general distribution of decisions. For the most part, the common law that applies to employment relationships is the law of contracts, although there are also elements of the law of torts that can frame a dispute between an employee, the employer and, sometimes, individual representatives of the employer as well.

I note from the outset that, except as background, the common law has little or no application to unionized employees. With few exceptions, as soon as a worker is hired into a position that is part of the bargaining unit, the individual contract of employment is completely absorbed by the terms and conditions of employment set out in the collective agreement. The collective agreement then applies for the balance of the period of employment, including the termination of employment. Even simply as background, there are still important lessons to be learned from principles of the common law.

To the extent that it applies, the boundary created by the common law is that if the employer does not treat employees in accordance with the centuries-old expectations of the courts, then the employer may find itself at the receiving end of a legal action commenced by an employee, typically following the termination of the employment relationship. Such cases are normally referred to as "wrongful dismissals". Naturally, most employers in most cases would rather avoid the time and money associated with a legal action. For that reason, understanding the common law, and acting in a way that will minimize the possibility that a formal legal proceeding will come into play effectively creates a self-imposed boundary or restriction on management rights. In other words, in this context, management can do anything that it wants, but it is prudent to act in a manner that is less likely to motivate a dismissed employee to commence or pursue a legal action.

There are three significant components of the common law as it applies to your non-union employees. The first is that each non-union employee is employed under a contract of employment. The second and third components arise out of the expectation that employers should act as good corporate citizens: management should be reasonably fair and frank in its representation of the key facts of employment, both at the outset of an employment relationship and whenever significant changes are made; furthermore, management should treat employees with reasonable dignity and respect at the time that the employment relationship is terminated, especially if it is terminated by a unilateral decision of management. In the last five years, this third component has led to a particular kind of claim, called *Wallace* damages, named after the 1997 decision of the Supreme Court of Canada that gave birth to the concept: *Wallace v. United Grain Growers Limited* [1997] 3 S.C.R. 701.

For unionized employees, the first component, which is the contract, is represented by the collective agreement. The second component may well apply to unionized employees, at least within the context of the collective agreement, but possibly as an independent right that employees cannot be subject to misrepresentations. The third component finds its parallel in the commonly applied expectation that management will exercise discretion and apply its rights in a reasonable manner that is not discriminatory, arbitrary or an exercise in bad faith.

The Law of Contracts

The first and fundamental component of the common law that applies to non-union employees comes from the law of contracts. A contract is typically between two parties. It deals with an exchange, where each party gives to the other party something of value. The contract is formed by a bargain that is initiated by the offer of one party and concluded by the acceptance of the other party, so long as each side considers that it has benefited from whatever is exchanged between the parties. There are often significant terms and conditions to ensure that the aspects of the exchange retain value for each party for the duration of the contract.

Every employment relationship that exists in Canada between an individual and an employer, from the part-time clerk at the corner grocer to the president of the largest bank, is a contract. In the bargain that is struck between an employee and his or her employer, the individual person is trading physical and mental attributes (brawn and brains), in varying degrees, in return for the compensation package that comes with a job, as well as some degree of security in employment.

Many people think of a contract as a formal legal document, complete with red seals and signed by quill pens. It does not have to be like that. It does not have to be written or it could be that only part of the contract is in writing. It could be made up of different parts, with one part (such as a letter of hire) specifically addressed to the individual employee and other parts (such as a benefits booklet and employee rules) generally addressed to all employees. Whatever is written to the individual employee could be on the back of a napkin, a letter of hire or something more formal.

For unionized employees, the terms and conditions of the employment contract are the terms and conditions that are collectively bargained and contained in the collective agreement. As such, if there is a complaint about terms and conditions of employment, including the termination of employment, then those complaints have to be processed under the grievance and arbitration provision in the collective agreement. Unionized employees generally have no right to proceed with an employment claim in the courts.

For non-union employees, the most contentious part of an employment contract has to do with termination of employment. For unionized employees, it is more straightforward. Unless the employment is terminated for just cause (a disciplinary dismissal), or unless the employee resigns or retires, the employee will be entitled to what is provided under employment standards law unless there is a greater right or benefit provided by the collective agreement.

For non-union employees, the standard legal concept is that an employee is hired for an indefinite period. Unless there is a clear contractual provision, which almost certainly has to be in writing, it will be assumed that an employment relationship has no defined end. Indeed, if there is nothing in writing about termination of employment, and if nothing like that was ever discussed with the employee before hire, then a court would be prepared to imply that the duration of the contract is indefinite.

From what is written above, it will be apparent that it is possible to have a contract for a defined term or task (for both union and non-union employees). A defined term means that the employment is for an actual time period and might include a renewal provision. A defined task means that the employment is intended to continue for the duration of a particular event, like the installation of a piece of equipment or the implementation of a computer system, or the opening or closing of a plant. In most cases, written contracts for a defined term or task do not cause legal problems at the end of the contract (the termination of employment) unless the contracts are poorly drafted.

With a contract of indefinite hire, employment will terminate in one of the following ways (all of which have their parallels in the context of a unionized workplace):

- for cause, in which case the employer typically argues that the employee has engaged in misconduct that is so serious that it constitutes a fundamental breach; typically, this suggests behaviour that is grossly dishonest or disruptive, sometimes to the point of being violent and even criminal; it can also refer to poor performance, especially if that has been documented and the employee has had a chance to improve;
- due to frustration of contract, including death or serious illness or injury, in which case the employee is no longer capable of meeting its side of the employment bargain, to provide physical and mental attributes to the employer on a reasonably regular basis;
- due to business failure, in which case the employees may retain claims in respect of a business that is bankrupt or in receivership, as well as potential claims against directors or other participants in the failed business;

- due to a fundamental change in the employee's duties or in other terms and conditions of employment, including but not limited to compensation — this is typically referred to as constructive dismissal;
- due to the employee's own resignation or retirement;
- in accordance with a retirement policy that is actively enforced, even if the employee would prefer not to retire; or
- as a result of providing reasonable notice or pay in lieu of some or all of that notice.

Legal issues may arise in any case of termination of employment. The most common legal claims have to do with the calculation of reasonable notice. In most cases, this really means a dispute about how much the employer has to pay in lieu of reasonable notice. Other common legal arguments arise when an employer claims cause for immediate termination of employment without compensation, or when an employee claims that s/he has been constructively dismissed.

It is important to understand that in most Canadian jurisdictions, subject to certain statutory claims, an employer is within its rights to terminate the employment of a non-union employee. When we talk of wrongful dismissal claims, it is not the dismissal itself that is wrongful. Rather, the wrong that is at the base of such a claim is that the employer did not give enough notice (or pay in lieu of notice), or, in cases of cause, frustration or constructive dismissal, that the employer did not give any notice.

It should be noted as well that a non-union employee could not make a common law claim and then simply sit back and wait for the money to roll in. The law expects that an employee, once terminated from active employment, will make every reasonable effort to find new employment. This is described as the obligation to mitigate damages. If an employee finds other employment, or if the employee fails to make reasonable efforts, then the employer involved in the termination of employment is entitled to an offset to the extent that the mitigation overlaps with the period of reasonable notice.

Indeed, even in the unionized context, mitigation is an important concept. An employee who has been discharged cannot simply file a grievance and hope for reinstatement with full back-pay. A discharged employee has to seek alternative employment actively. It may be several months before an arbitrator can rule on the propriety of the discharge. In the meantime, it is expected that most employees will be able to offset their losses with other earnings.

The Law of Torts

The second applicable component of the common law comes from the law of torts. The law of torts has to do with how people treat each other. Unlike a contract, where two parties make an agreement to deal with each other in a certain way, the law of torts deals with common expectations and understandings that do not need to be part of specific agreements between people. In a civilized society, we expect that people will act in good faith, without violence, and with a proper respect for the property of other people. If these expectations are not met, individual offenders can be criminally prosecuted. They can also be the subjects of a separate civil lawsuit.

In the United States, an example of the two different proceedings, criminal and civil, can be found in the notorious O.J. Simpson case. Mr. Simpson, a professional football player, was acquitted of criminal charges related to the death of his wife Nicole and a man named Ronald Goldman. The family of Mr. Goldman subsequently commenced a civil lawsuit that was successful, in which they claimed that Mr. Simpson had wrongfully caused the death of Mr. Goldman and should be liable to the family in damages for all of the losses that would be suffered because Mr. Goldman was no longer alive.

A tort is sometimes, but not necessarily, related to a crime. Many torts involve misconduct that could not be the subject of a criminal prosecution, but which is still widely expected to be subject to sanctions if other people are harmed as a direct and foreseeable consequence of the poor behaviour. In employment situations, employees could commence a legal action against the employer and, as we will see, sometimes other employees as well.

The law of torts has not been particularly significant in the employment context to date, but there have been some high profile and noteworthy court decisions, especially in the past twenty years. As a result, claims arising from the manner in which an employee has been treated, as opposed to the law of the employment contract, may become much more prominent in the future. This is certainly likely for non-union employees. Whether or not there is ever much application to unionized employees matters less than the lessons that all workplaces should take from these concepts of tort law.

The basic concept is the expectation of reasonable and frank representation of key facts of employment. The courts expect truth, or at least the avoidance of deceit, and a certain degree of diligence when it comes to making representations about a job. It is not enough for employer representatives to be honest, they must also be reasonably well informed, so that they do not "honestly" misrepresent key facts because of a lack of knowledge.

Just as a house built on sand is doomed to fall, an employment relationship is fundamentally flawed if it is based on deceit, misstatements, misleading information or recklessness on the part of the employer or its representative. Indeed, even if there is a written contract of employment in such a situation, it may be voided by the courts, entitling the employee to significant remedies under both tort law and contract law without regard to the written document.

If a representative of the employer holds out that s/he has the authority to enter into an employment contract on behalf of the employer, then a special relationship is created with the job applicant in the context of the hiring process. This is also true for existing employees in situations of promotion or re-assignment. Representatives who are decision-makers or who act in that manner have to expect that the targets of their representations will act on the basis of the statements made (and perhaps the information concealed) by the representatives. There is a special duty of care to be respected by these employer representatives. In enforcing this special duty, the courts take account of the fact that there is relatively little cost in ensuring that managers who hire or promote are working from a base of carefully prepared and correct information. By contrast, it would be extremely costly, if not impossible in many instances, for employees or prospective hires to verify the accuracy of the representations made by these managers.

A careful representative must not represent material facts to the employee or prospective hire if the representative knows, or ought to know, that the facts are wrong or misleading. No person can be expected to know the future; however, if the present reality of a company is materially different from what is represented to an employee or prospective hire, then it may be the foundation for a claim for damages. For example, if an applicant for a position at a plant in Toronto inquires about whether or not the plant is likely to remain stable or in a growth mode, then it could be a negligent misrepresentation to provide such reassurance when there are in fact active plans to close the plant.

The law has little interest in cases where no real harm is done.To have a valid claim, the applicant in our Toronto plant example must act on the basis of the representation. The applicant must rely on the representation to his or her detriment. The reliance must be reasonable. A clear example of reasonable and detrimental reliance would be if the applicant were to leave secure and long-term employment only to find out six months later that the plant is closing. On the other hand, it likely would not be reasonable for an applicant to rely on information that the applicant knows to be untrue or at least questionable.

Law is dynamic. As this area of the law evolves, it may be that there will be not only a prohibition against deceit and negligent misstatement, but also a requirement to make representations about relevant facts that are within the knowledge of the employer, but would not be obvious to a prospective employee. Using the same example of the doomed Toronto plant, it may be that a job applicant has to be told about the likely future of the plant even if there is no such inquiry initiated by the applicant. Indeed, it may be that representatives of an employer who have recruitment and hiring responsibilities have to engage in ongoing due diligence about their own companies to ensure that current information about the employer that is relevant is communicated to a job applicant in a timely and proactive manner. Naturally, any such legal principle will depend on such particular facts as the position and the legitimate expectations of the prospective employee, as well as the degree of certainty of the information in question. You can imagine how tricky this could become if the decision about the plant is not final, or is not general knowledge. The courts are often required to strike a balance. In this case, the balance would be between the interest of the employee or the prospective hire in being able to make rational career decisions and the employer's interest in protecting its confidential information and in keeping the costs of preparing such information within reasonable bounds.

In any event, and subject to the peculiarities that exist with any unique set of facts, the general rule for employers should be that their representatives should conduct themselves in a manner that is always honest and reasonably frank and complete. This should be so in meetings with employees and prospective employees, and also in terms of the disclosure of material facts and information in situations of hire or promotion. Dishonesty and evasion could lead to exposure, not only for the employer, but also, on an individual basis, for the representative who is the cause of the problem. This could be particularly important in the event that a company has financial problems, as the dishonest or negligent representative could remain directly liable for damage as an individual defendant.

The consequences of reckless or dishonest behaviour on behalf of representatives of the employer could be dire. There could be damages for lost income and job search expenses while the employee finds other employment, as well as losses suffered from relocation if the employee moved in order to take the job in the first place or s/he has to move to find new employment. There also could be damages for emotional distress. As far as existing employees are concerned, there could be damages for lost opportunities if an employee chooses to continue employment as a result of statements made by a representative of the employer that are reckless or known by the representative to be untrue. Contractual concepts like probationary periods or specified notice periods or severance payments are irrelevant to these kinds of claims, whether by new hires or existing employees, and would have no limiting effect on the damages that could be claimed.

It is possible contractually to create a disclaimer that takes away the employer's responsibility for the truth of any representations made and puts the burden entirely on the new hire to be satisfied about the soundness of the employment relationship. At the very least, this disclaimer must be clearly and comprehensively drafted, and it should be brought to the new hire's attention before or simultaneously with making the representations, and certainly before employment is actually commenced. Having raised the possibility of such a disclaimer, I must comment that it is a poor start to an employment relationship to tell an employee that s/he should not rely on the representations that are being made by the manager responsible for recruitment and hiring. A court will have little sympathy for the employer in such a situation and would delight in finding flaws in the drafting or hiring process, such that a contractual disclaimer would not invalidate a claim in tort.

It is important for employer representatives not to be unduly fearful as a result of this discussion of the consequences of deceit or negligent misstatements. These are not trivial matters and claims cannot be founded on a base of normal communications. Employer representatives are entitled to be optimistic and opinionated about the employer. Expectations of future growth and prosperity are not deceitful and do not constitute negligent misstatements just because the anticipated or hoped for growth does not materialize, unless the expectations arise from assumptions that have no reasonable basis in fact. The concern is with present-day facts, which have to be honestly represented and reasonably factored into assumptions and future forecasts. The courts have no concern with rosy futures that do not come to pass as a result of future events that could not have been foreseen. Representatives can still be enthusiastic salespersons. The courts do not expect representatives to be prophets or to have reliable crystal balls.

Although employers are most vulnerable with non-union employees, given that the normal expectation is that unionized employees should pursue their claims through the grievance and arbitration procedure, there are two points worth noting:

1. At least to the extent that claims in tort could be made against individuals, the possibility remains that unionized employees could pursue a legal claim in the courts; and
2. In any event, you can be assured that arbitrators and labour relations boards have at least the same expectation of fair representations and honest dealing; indeed, it is perhaps even more highly developed.

Wallace Damages

The third component that is directly relevant to non-union employees and a benchmark for unionized employees is a gloss that has been added to the common law of contracts. As a result of the *Wallace* decision, the conduct of an employer at the point of dismissal may affect a court's assessment of the damages owing to the employee.

As discussed above, in the absence of just cause and in the absence of an express contractual provision dealing with termination of employment, an employee is generally entitled to receive reasonable notice of dismissal. Absent such notice, there is typically entitlement to damages in lieu of reasonable notice to compensate for the breach.

In the last twenty years, the courts have been encouraged by lawyers for employees to loosen the stranglehold of the traditional contractual notion of reasonable notice. Plaintiffs have sought aggravated damages for mental distress caused by the dismissal. Defendant employers have presented a variety of obstacles to such claims, including causation, remoteness, medical proof of mental distress and limitations in the courts' ability to make reasonable inferences as to the intention of the parties in framing the contract. In the result, there were increasingly artificial legal arguments built more on hyperbole than on facts or a logical legal analysis.

With *Wallace*, the Supreme Court of Canada tried to cut through the nonsense while at the same time holding employers accountable for the dismissal process. The Court made it clear that aggravated damages may only be awarded to a plaintiff where the acts of the employer or its representatives that gave rise to the injury were independently actionable. The failure to give reasonable notice is not, itself, likely to be sufficient to cause mental distress. Courts must be shown something more, such as a verbal or physical assault or a fraudulent misrepresentation.

Having made it more difficult for a plaintiff to claim aggravated damages, the Supreme Court of Canada in *Wallace* then provided plaintiffs with a way around the issue. The employer is probably not required as a matter of contract to act fairly and in good faith in making dismissal decisions, and the act of dismissal by itself does not likely create a tort. That said, and probably as a matter of public policy more than legal theory, the Court determined that the period of reasonable notice could be extended in situations when the employer demonstrates bad faith or dismisses an employee in an unfair manner that causes mental suffering for the employee. In other words, if the employee can provide compelling evidence of mental suffering on the one hand and bad conduct by the employer on the other, the employee does not have to worry about the legal obstacles that employers have relied on in defence of claims for aggravated damages.

Although it has cleared up much of the mess caused by the push for aggravated damages, *Wallace* has introduced a new element of uncertainty and a potential for judicial creativity that has not been welcome news for employers. Absent a clear contractual provision, calculating damages in lieu of reasonable notice always has been more art than science. Now it is more so. Plaintiffs now routinely claim *Wallace* damages on even the flimsiest facts, which creates one more bargaining chip and one more obstacle in the settlement process.

Although the law is not entirely settled in this respect, it is at least arguable that *Wallace* has no application in cases where the notice period is contractually specified. That is, when the employer has entered into a pre-employment or (less clearly) a pre-promotion contract with a new hire or employee that sets out the notice period or payments to be made in the event of dismissal, then the courts should have no role to play in determining the reasonable period of notice. As such, the use of well defined notice periods in written employment contracts should become increasingly popular with employers wishing to prevent the courts from using *Wallace* to increase the period of reasonable notice. Unfortunately for employers, given what I consider to be a rather uncertain legal basis for the policy-driven *Wallace* doctrine, I expect that the courts will remain open to invitations to apply *Wallace* even in the face of a clearly drafted written contract.

The Second Boundary — Statutory Law

Even after centuries of evolution, judge-made law had at least a couple of major drawbacks. First, a court could only deal with the particular set of facts that would come before it in each case. This kind of scattershot evolution led to holes in the law, as well as inconsistencies between cases. Second, as there was no real plan or rulebook, the common law did not naturally take a leadership role in building a just society.

Statutory law is the law that is made by elected politicians. Statutory law began to have a significant impact on workplaces in the latter part of the nineteenth century, after the first few generations of industrial revolution in Europe, and with the rapid evolution of the new democracies in North America. Most of the important statutory law that affects our workplaces has been developed since World War II.

In Canada, employment law in its statutory form is made primarily by provincial legislatures. The federal government has fairly narrow jurisdiction that covers federal institutions and organizations like banks, telecommunication companies, cable companies, and companies involved in inter-provincial transportation (not an exhaustive list). Provincial governments are responsible for almost all activity in manufacturing, mining, construction and most of the service industries.

Statutory law is a significant tool that governments can use in order to put their political agendas into effect. By its nature, statutory law allows political parties elected to power to change fundamental rules that govern society. Statutory law can fill in the holes left by the common law and smooth out real and perceived inequities or inconsistencies.

The five most significant areas of statutory law in the workplace are:

1. Employment standards — these standards set the floor for workplaces in Canada, such that you have to meet at least the minimum statutory requirements in order to operate a business; most businesses exceed the minimum standards to a significant degree.

2. Labour law, or the law of trade unions — this is the law that determines how a trade union gets certified to act as the sole and exclusive agent for a group of employees, what obligations are thereby created for the employer of those employees, and what is the framework to govern the relationship between the union and the employer in respect of the affected group of employees.

3. Health and safety — there is an internal responsibility system in Canada that places the obligation on the various workplace players to co-exist and co-operate in a safe and healthy workplace environment; this is achieved in large part by providing worker representatives and health and safety committees with significant powers to become informed and to bring unsafe or unhealthy conditions to the attention of the employer.

4. Workers' compensation or workplace safety and insurance — this is the insurance system run by the various provincial governments that provides a complex system of benefits to workers who are injured or who become ill because of workplace situations, in return for which workers give up the right to sue their employers for creating the unsafe or unhealthy situation or for allowing it to continue in existence.

5. Human rights, including laws dealing with equity in pay and employment — this is the relatively recent area of workplace law that has become a fundamental force in the western world following World War II; essentially this area of the law mandates that people must be hired and promoted in the workplace without regard to such external characteristics as race, culture, gender, age, or even handicap.

Statutory law has created powerful administrative tribunals, bureaucracies and civil servants, including labour relations boards, human rights commissions, health and safety inspectors, employment standards officers and workers' compensation boards.

Let us take a closer look at how each of the above areas of statutory law creates restrictions on the rights of management to do whatever it wants in operating the workplace. The intention is not to provide a mini-review of each area of legislative intervention. Rather, the main objective is to gain an understanding of the nature of the restrictions on management rights in each area.

Employment Standards

The floor plan created by employment standards legislation covers the fundamental terms and conditions of any employment relationship, although often at a very basic level. Much of the time spent in negotiating a collective agreement is essentially a result of the union seeking improvements on terms and conditions that appear at a basic level in the governing employment standards law.

On the compensation side, a minimum wage is established, but there is little or no guidance provided in respect of benefits or pension plans. Statutory holiday and vacation entitlements are set out. There are detailed pregnancy leave rights, and other unpaid leaves may be described. Significant obligations are created for situations of termination of employment or lengthy lay-offs, although short-term lay-offs are not covered. There are also important obligations established for employers to maintain records. The employment standards bureaucracy is given the usual powers of investigation, and each statute has a mechanism for the adjudication of disputes, although it may be expected or required that bargaining unit employees will have their statutory claims addressed in the grievance and arbitration procedure and not through the statutory framework.

Employment standards legislation should be used at the front end and the back end of any framework for human resources management, with the collective agreement(s) at the front and centre of any unionized workplace. At the front end, the basic elements of employment standards legislation are a good starting point for the framework. At the back end, it is important to check the framework against employment standards requirements to ensure that nothing has been missed and nothing is offside.

Labour Law, the Law of Trade Unions

There are two key parts to the statutory law dealing with trade unions. The first part describes how a trade union acquires the legal right to represent employees in a workplace — this is the process of certification. The second part sets out a trade union's rights and an employer's obligations once the trade union is certified — the most important of these deals with the negotiation of the collective agreement. The collective agreement is a written deal between the employer and union that covers the terms and conditions of employment, which thereby forms the contractual framework within which the employer, the employees, and the union representatives must operate. The collective agreement is, in effect, the private legislation of the workplace, designed to limit the exercise of management rights.

Through direct negotiations, the parties establish the provisions of the collective agreement. However, if the parties are unable to reach agreement through direct negotiations, they generally have recourse to a lawful strike/lockout in accordance with labour relations legislation. A lawful work stoppage will continue until such time as the parties resume negotiations to resolve any outstanding issues and thereby establish a new collective agreement.

Naturally, a unionized employer is no longer much concerned about the first part, which is how a union gets organized — you are pretty much stuck with the second part, which focuses on the creation of the collective agreement.

Establishing Bargaining Rights: As to the first part, which deals with the establishment of a union's bargaining rights, the starting point is the notion of a bargaining unit and a trade union representative of the unit. For the most part, the bargaining unit consists of a grouping of workers of a single employer, either at a single location or within a geographical area that is typically the size of a municipality, county, or something similar. It is typical to group blue-collar workers separately from white-collar workers. As well, there are certain trades or professions, like operating engineers, nurses and security guards, which have their own distinct units, either by law or by historical convention. Management employees are excluded from bargaining units, as are workers with confidential functions related to labour relations; however, the dividing line can vary from jurisdiction to jurisdiction and even from case to case.

If you have multiple plants or offices within a municipality-like geographical area, and some of them, or some parts of them, remain non-union, then you have to be aware of the potential for additional union organizing. If one of your existing unions is successful, you could end up with a grouping of employees that extends to your multiple locations, although you remain vulnerable as well to any union at each individual location.

If you are frustrated because labour law makes it easy for trade unions to organize, your frustration is exactly the point. It is supposed to be easy. So long as a trade union has the majority support of a group of workers that is viable for purposes of collective bargaining, the law takes the view that a unionized workplace is preferable and that workers should be entitled to union representation.

All jurisdictions in Canada allow for organizing drives, in which trade unions attempt to have employees sign union membership cards. Membership at this stage costs little or nothing. In some jurisdictions, all that a union has to do is to sign up enough employees in the bargaining unit and that will suffice for the certificate. In other jurisdictions, notably Ontario, signing cards is a necessary precondition to a representation vote, but the union requires the support of the majority of those who vote in a secret-ballot election before a certificate will be granted.

In all jurisdictions, an employer must conduct itself during an organizing drive with reasonable restraint. Neither threats to job security nor promises of better compensation in return for the union's defeat are acceptable. A union can raise allegations of misconduct at the Labour Relations Board, which has wide remedial powers, which vary from jurisdiction to jurisdiction. Free speech is still the hallmark of our democracy, so an employer retains significant rights of expression during the organizing campaign. Indeed, those rights have been significantly reinforced in Ontario in recent years, so that even if an employer engages in misconduct, a union will not be granted bargaining rights unless it can win a secret ballot vote — there is no automatic certification in Ontario.

Because labour laws can change quickly and quite dramatically, and because there are important differences from jurisdiction to jurisdiction, it is generally important at the stage of a union organizing campaign to retain legal counsel to help you design a campaign of appropriate response to an organizing drive and to make judgment calls about the legality of specific actions. Law is rarely black or white; it comes in many shades of grey. That is particularly true when it comes to making determinations about the limits to be respected by an employer in the face of an aggressive organizing drive.

If a union is successful in achieving a certificate, it is thereafter recognized as the sole and exclusive bargaining agent for a defined group of employees. In the result, unions represent workers who actively campaigned against them, as well as new workers who were never involved in the organizing campaign and who never make an individual choice about whether or not they want a union. Indeed, in time, a workplace will become full of workers who did not actually choose the union. Most of these will be relatively apathetic about the ongoing role of the union. Some will become active supporters and others will remain hostile, either to this particular union or to unions in general.

Terminating Bargaining Rights: Although there are processes to terminate the bargaining rights of a union, it is very difficult to get rid of a union once it has been certified. Even with the democratic right of free speech, employers are particularly limited in their ability to influence or support employees who may wish to terminate bargaining rights. Any kind of employer involvement in the decertification process is usually fatal. As a result, even if a union is not very popular with the workers, it takes an unusual combination of leadership, knowledge, courage and motivation before there can be any real threat to a union.

What may be more likely is that one union will raid another, although there are restrictions on such raids for unions that are affiliated with the Canadian Labour Congress. Whether because of a raid or a decertification, applications can take place only at the end of a collective agreement or if the union fails in its efforts to achieve an agreement.

Collective Bargaining: With a certified trade union in place, we turn to the second part of labour legislation. In all jurisdictions, the employer and the union must bargain in good faith with a view to achieving a collective agreement. This certainly does not mean that either side has to be a pushover. Indeed, the employer is well within its rights to engage in hard bargaining. Although unions like to promise prospective members that the terms and conditions of employment can only improve with a first collective agreement, the employer is not legally compelled to make improvements. Indeed, with business justification, an employer can lawfully seek concessions in a first agreement. Certainly in subsequent agreements, although the union will aggressively challenge it, an employer can lawfully seek concessions.

Bargaining in good faith also does not restrict the normal tactics that can be found in any kind of negotiations. While the parties should not be blatantly dishonest with each other, bluffs, feints, straw targets, and secret strategies are quite acceptable. A bluff consists of threatening a consequence without necessarily meaning to follow through if the bluff is called. A feint is when you appear to be moving in a certain direction, while you may simply be trying to extract information from the other side, mislead them, or compel them to abandon or alter a position. A straw target is when you try to make the other side believe that you have one objective when you really have a different objective; if you bargain hard for something you have no real interest in achieving, you can sometimes pave the way to winning something different or more modest that may have been difficult to achieve in isolation. Secret strategies are fundamental to labour negotiations, in that you should never fully reveal your final position on any issue so that, even at the end, the other side is left guessing as to whether or not you left it all on the table.

What is really meant by bargaining in good faith is that you make efforts to achieve a collective agreement that you can live with. This generally means that you have a starting point and an end point, which I typically refer to as the "drop-dead" point. Negotiations generally consist of each party moving from its starting point to its drop-dead point in a way that brings the two parties closer together. If you are moving farther apart, then good faith is probably rightly questioned, unless there have been intervening events that would justify an altered position. For this reason, it is generally not a good practice to have a "take-it or-leave-it" position from the outset of negotiations, either on individual issues or on the entire package. That may be an effective closing technique, but it generally belongs at the end of negotiations, not the beginning.

It is good practice to think of negotiations like a chess game or like a book. There is an opening phase, in which the starting positions are identified. There is the middle phase, where most of the movement or action takes place. There is, at the end, a closing phase, where you move from playing the game or developing the plot to ending it: you either win the game or at least you try to achieve a resolution. Many negotiations actually proceed in two phases, where first you try to resolve language items, and then start all over again with the monetary items — compensation and language items that carry a price tag.

Success in negotiations requires that the drop-dead points of each party overlap. Because neither side is likely to reveal their drop-dead point, and certainly should not do so at the outset of negotiations, much of the process is spent in trying to figure out just how far the other side will go. If they go far enough to be acceptable to you, even if you are not overjoyed with the result, then you likely will achieve a settlement. Labour negotiations can become complicated because the drop-dead point on one or more other issues may influence the drop-dead point on any particular issue. It is for this reason that the parties typically try to deal with language items first to shrink the table. When it comes time to deal with monetary items, most employers promote a concept of total compensation, so that they are really dealing with one issue — the size of the pie.

Assuming that each side is negotiating in good faith and with some reasonable understanding about how to go about it, then you should achieve a settlement unless the ultimate drop-dead points do not overlap. That is, if the employer's best position is still not good enough for the union, then you will reach an impasse.

If collective bargaining breaks down, then a legal strike or lockout will, in most cases, follow a government supervised conciliation process. Most such work stoppages eventually end in a settlement, although often not until several weeks have passed. The whole point of the work stoppage is to force one side or the other or both to change their drop-dead points so that overlap is achieved and a settlement zone is created.

Some work stoppages lead to a complete breakdown in the relationship, which may result in a shutdown of the operation or an ongoing stalemate. In some situations and some sectors a breakdown in collective bargaining will lead to "interest" arbitration, in which a neutral adjudicator will determine the outstanding issues and thereby settle the collective agreement.

Health and Safety

It is a moral duty, as well as a legal requirement, that employers in Canada co-operate with their employees in order to operate safe and healthy workplaces. It is unfortunate that this is an obligation that is much clearer and more keenly felt after a serious accident. It is important to embrace healthy and safe practices from the earliest possible opportunity. A very useful strategy is to look for "near-misses", where no worker is hurt but there could have been injuries with either bad luck or bad timing. If you can find or create near-misses, then you can use those to teach healthy and safe practices in a very meaningful manner.

For unionized workplaces, health and safety law provides an ideal opportunity to try to break through the adversarial relationship and create co-operation between workers and management. Any opportunity you can create and reinforce "us", you make it more difficult for a union to move you away from achieving management objectives. In this respect you should be absolutely committed to a safe and healthy workplace as a fundamental management objective. Not only is that a legal imperative, it makes good business sense and, in particular, is key to effective human resources management.

As a matter of law, management and workers are required to co-operate in creating and maintaining a healthy and safe workplace. The internal responsibility system, which is the basis for Canadian health and safety law, places the onus on the workplace participants to create a good working environment. The role of government is to resolve disputes and to ensure that the system is functioning as it should; otherwise, the system features self-monitoring, self-improvement and self-regulation for the most part. Workers are entitled to have input through regular inspections and committee meetings. They are entitled to make recommendations through meeting minutes that must be considered by the employer. Workers can properly expect management to respond in an effective and timely fashion to reasonable suggestions for improving the workplace environment. Unions will typically feature health and safety as an issue to be promoted in each round of collective bargaining. From a union's standpoint, whatever has been achieved to this point can always be improved for the future.

Sensible employers should try to take the lead in matters of health and safety. Although it is a shared responsibility and there is tremendous scope for worker input, it is ultimately the employer and the members of the management team that will bear responsibility in the event of a serious accident or fatality. As a result, it is important for the employer to maintain a comprehensive and current safety policy, to implement procedures for safe operation and dealing with accidents or unsafe incidents, to teach safe practices, and to impose rules against unsafe practices with disciplinary consequences. Consistent with the co-operative nature of health and safety, worker input is very helpful in all of these respects and is probably the best way to raise the profile of health and safety in the workplace. Indeed, effective and ongoing opportunities for input in the development of policies, procedures and rules can result in the employees training themselves to a significant extent.

Safety is a hot button issue. Regardless of the best efforts of unionized employers, it is likely to be featured in any round of collective bargaining, as well as in the ongoing relationship with the union. You can never get rid of safety as an issue. You can never erase the memory of a serious accident. The best you can do is to focus on health and safety issues with serious intent, and to demonstrate continuously to your workers and to their union that you are prepared to listen to their concerns and ideas, and to take action that is appropriate and reasonable.

Workers' Compensation

Workers' compensation (workplace safety and insurance in Ontario) is really the flip side of health and safety law. To the extent that accidents occur in a workplace, or illnesses develop, there is a decades-old insurance scheme (since as early as 1915 in Ontario) that provides benefits to workers on the one hand and, on the other hand, protects employers from employee lawsuits.

Increasingly, workers' compensation is not simply a system for compensating workers who become ill or injured as a result (at least in part) of workplace activities. Workers' compensation has become focused on rehabilitation of injured workers and returning them to active employment, preferably at their former workplaces. An employer has legal obligations to accommodate such workers.

If workers are absent from the workplace due to illness or injury, then management should closely track the progress of the worker and aggressively seek out opportunities to return the worker to the workplace as quickly as possible. It is common for a worker to come back to modified work and even modified hours. There may be a work-trial period typically lasting four to eight weeks, during which the worker can get up to speed, either at his or her former job or at a suitably modified job that is still useful to the employer. An employer can enhance its reputation and stature with the workers by demonstrating compassion and flexibility. At the same time, an employer must not lose sight of the disruptive and negative impact that modified work can have on the workplace if it is not properly and diligently managed. Dissension breeds fastest if there is a sense of injustice between employees, where some think that others are getting away with a lighter load.

Modified work exacts a price, on the employer, the worker in question and co-workers. The employer is, hopefully, still getting reasonable productivity from the worker, but less than optimal productivity. The worker is unable to work at his or her full potential and may well be suffering some income loss as a result. Co-workers may have to shoulder both inconvenience and heavier or more difficult work. Alternatively, co-workers may lose the opportunity to access job vacancies that involve lighter work and perhaps even higher pay, as preference for those positions may be given to workers with disabilities. As a result, the general rule is that modified work should be viewed as temporary. Every effort should be made to return the worker to full or regular duties as soon as possible. Failure to do so by the employer could have a negative impact on the morale of the work force and could breed dissension, especially if it becomes a pattern and is not isolated to infrequent situations.

If it becomes apparent that permanent modifications are necessary, because the worker has reached a point of maximum medical recovery, then it is important that the employer look at re-organizing the workplace in a permanent way to accommodate the disability. Such re-organization has to be effective for both the employer and the worker. It is generally necessary to involve the union at this stage. Stopgap solutions that may be appropriate for a short period of work-trial or for a temporary period while medical recovery is ongoing are rarely appropriate in the longer term. Indeed, in some cases, and subject to a close analysis of human rights and workers' compensation requirements, it may be determined that permanent accommodation is not possible.

In many workplaces, employers are sharing the burden of these issues with the union by setting up modified work and return-to-work committees with union participation. These committees may be the product of collective bargaining or may be set up with the union separate and apart from negotiations.

In addition to aggressive return-to-work initiatives, a second key element of managing workers' compensation is the need for accurate and timely reporting. Workers need to be able to trust management. They need to know that, if they have a claim, management will view it as a priority to report promptly and completely. Similarly, if management has doubts about an injury or illness, they owe it to all other employees to raise those doubts in a frank and fair manner, with appropriate opportunity for response. If workers get a sense that their fellow workers are able to play with the system, then the integrity of the system will be seriously harmed and other workers may be tempted to abuse it.

Workplaces that do a poor job of balancing the interests of injured workers who are returning to work with the interests of other workers in the plant are vulnerable to grievances either on behalf of the injured worker or the others, whichever way the imbalance tilts. Whether or not there is a return to work involved, unions, with some justification, can portray themselves as expert advocates for injured workers. At the same time, especially if modified work is required, unions can reassure the other workers that, through the collective agreement, and the active participation of union representatives in such areas as modified work, accommodation, ergonomics and health and safety, the workplace can be made a better and more equitable place for all workers.

Human Rights

We have already introduced some human rights issues in dealing with the rehabilitation and return to work of injured workers. Essentially, human rights law for workplace purposes is divided into two parts: discrimination and harassment. The prohibitions against discrimination are based on the notion that an employer should recruit, hire and promote without regard to external characteristics, focusing only on the real skills, abilities and qualifications of each person. The prohibitions against harassment are based in the notion that all persons should be free from abuse from co-workers and supervisors that arises from their external characteristics, gender and race or culture in particular.

Discrimination can arise directly, due to the improper conduct and attitudes of decision-makers. It also can be indirect or constructive in nature, insofar as it arises from barriers to effective recruitment, hiring and promotion practices. For example, if an employer recruits through word-of-mouth referrals from existing employees, then such an employer is simply perpetuating the existing social, economic and cultural makeup of the organization. Potentially, you could be missing out on significant groups in your community that may have qualified and motivated candidates for employment. If you have tests or physical qualifications that are not reasonably related to the work for which you are hiring, then you may be screening out applicants who are perfectly capable. If you value paper qualifications over work experience in promotion situations, then you may be missing out on skilled workers who have not succeeded in formal schooling or training because of learning disabilities that would not impact on the quality or quantity of their work. Some of these misplaced barriers may be illegal as contrary to human rights legislation; others may be simply bad for business.

Failure to prevent harassment between employees can lead to a poisoned workplace. Unhappily, the workers who tend to leave such an environment are the victims. The employer who has not controlled the workplace could be stuck with the bigoted, sexist or simply ignorant creeps who have engaged in the misconduct in the first place. Remember basic management rights: you have the right to create the workplace that you want. By law, you have the obligation to prevent harassment. Racial humour, sexual banter and innuendo, graphic posters, and crude language do not need to have any place in your workplace if you say so. You set the standard. Here, the standard should be set high and there should be little tolerance for contravention of the standard. That is what the law expects of management. You have the right, and probably the obligation, to insist on a civil workplace.

A union has similar obligations under the law. For the most part, protecting human rights and preventing harassment is an area for significant co-operation between employers and unions. This is both as it should be, and as it must be, given the legal expectations of all parties in the workplace.

Puritanical zeal is not required. Indeed, excessive reactions by management may compel an otherwise co-operative union to file grievances to protect those engaged in the misconduct, even though the union may have little sympathy for the grievor. Nobody expects or even wants your workplace to be cleansed of shoptalk, friendly banter, and normal human interaction. There is a line, however, and for the most part, it is a pretty bright line. Usually, crossing the line is obvious and it should not be tolerated. Victims of misconduct deserve to be protected. Those who are unwilling to respect the dignity and self-worth of co-workers should be disciplined and, if necessary, dismissed.

Naturally, you will have little hope of enforcing standards that discourage harassment if your supervisors and managerial staff are not prepared to provide leadership in this area. The law recognizes two particular forms of managerial misconduct in relation to sex: solicitation and reprisal. These are really two sides of the same coin. In each case, a person who is in a position to confer or deny a benefit uses his (it is for the most part not "her") influence in an effort to gain a sexual advantage. Solicitation involves a promise of a benefit, such as a raise, time off or a promotion, in return for a sexual favour. Reprisal involves the threat of loss if a sexual favour is not granted or as payback for being spurned. The most obvious loss would be the job itself, but there are many less obvious consequences that an authority figure could visit upon a subordinate worker that could be devastating in their cumulative effect. An employer should have little or no tolerance for supervisors who engage in solicitation or reprisal activities.

For the most part, engaging in effective human rights practices is good for the proper conduct of business in your organization and it should make you a stronger group. As with health and safety, unionized workplaces should find much common ground between employers and unions in keeping the workplace free from discrimination and harassment.

The Third Boundary — The Collective Agreement

With statutory law, trade unions can acquire the right to represent a group of employees and to compel the employer to bargain a collective agreement that would set out the fundamental terms and conditions of employment. Further, such other statutory laws as employment standards, occupational health and safety, workers' compensation and human rights create the framework for the terms and conditions that appear in the collective agreement.

EFFECTIVE HR MANAGEMENT IN THE UNION ENVIRONMENT

Whether settled through consensual bargaining, conciliation, mediation, impasse bargaining during a work stoppage or arbitration, and whether required by law or expected by convention, almost all collective agreements share these common characteristics:

1. recognition of the union as the bargaining agent for a defined group of employees;
2. recognition of management rights, except as restricted by the collective agreement or law;
3. automatic deduction of union dues;
4. recognition of union representatives;
5. prohibition against work stoppages during the term of the collective agreement;
6. a term of at least one year and typically two or three years, sometimes longer; note that by the time some collective agreements are settled, the term is already partially or even completely over and it is time to start negotiations all over again;
7. seniority provisions, including clauses dealing with promotions and lay-offs;
8. provisions dealing with scheduling of work, including hours of work, overtime, and premium time, such as weekends and night shifts;
9. vacation, holiday and leave provisions;
10. compensation, including classifications, wages, perquisites, benefits, and sometimes pension plans; and
11. a formal procedure to deal with complaints, called the grievance procedure, including access to arbitration as the final stage for resolution of disputes.

Collective agreements contain a significant number and variety of provisions that do not contradict an efficient and effective operation. In many cases, a unionized workplace ends up as a more efficiently managed workplace. It is also very important to understand that the collective agreement is only one boundary on management rights and is far from being entirely restrictive. Indeed, as noted above in point 2 in the above list, management rights are specifically recognized as continued, subject to the specific restrictions in the collective agreement. That means that management can continue to make rules and policies, establish practices, and react to performance issues, whether positive or negative.

The Fourth Boundary — Self-Imposed Boundaries

For our purposes, the self-imposed boundaries are not obvious ones, such as capital budgets, cash flow, and the overall purpose of the production or services in which the organization is engaged. Rather, we are talking about such key employment concepts as policies, procedures, practices, rules, culture and history of the workplace. Let us take a closer look at how these are distinctive and yet work together as a cohesive whole.

Policies

Policies are those wide-reaching concepts of human resources management that are fundamental to the effective management of the work force. These are usually carefully considered, regularly reviewed, and written down in a formal manner. Some policies are either required by law or the collective agreement, or at least widely expected to be in place, such as safety, dealing with harassment, and avoiding discriminatory practices in situations of hiring and promotion. Other policies may include such issues as attendance management, discipline, job evaluation, seniority and training.

Procedures

Procedures are more mechanical than policies and involve the practical steps required to get things done, including implementation of the policies themselves. Procedures usually fall into two general categories. First, there are the procedures that are important to the employer in terms of producing the goods or providing the services that are fundamental to the objectives of the organization. Second, there are the procedures that are important to employees and their union in terms of getting the entitlements, benefits and perquisites that compensate the employees for the work they perform and that allow the employees to integrate work reasonably into the other aspects of their lives.

Some important procedures include all manner of operational issues, as well as dealing with employee complaints and grievances, calling in absences, performance evaluation, corrective action, filling job vacancies, applying for leaves, and vacation scheduling. Procedures should be written out in some descriptive fashion. Procedures are often accompanied by notices posted on bulletin boards or in other areas of the workplace, as well as by forms generated or controlled by HRP's.

Practices

Practices are often unwritten and largely unnoticed because they are so obvious and widespread. They are the daily, weekly and monthly routines that are straightforward and repetitive and that are predominant in the workplace. Practices deal with such everyday expectations as when employees should be at their work stations, when breaks are taken, how new work is assigned, how overtime is assigned, how absent employees are replaced, and how to deal with machine breakdowns and excessive scrap or unnecessary delays in providing services. In many cases, practices breathe life into collective agreement provisions. In some cases, they are contradictory. In either case, this could become important, as the practices may serve to amplify or even overwhelm provisions that were carefully negotiated, but not thoughtfully implemented.

Rules

Rules are specific and narrow. Whereas policies deal in a wide manner with big issues, rules deal with simple issues that can be understood quickly, with obvious consequences for non-compliance. Some examples of rules are:

- You must wear safety equipment
- You may not wear safety shoes or uniforms except at the workplace or for work purposes
- You must follow the procedures for safe operation of equipment
- You must not engage in horseplay
- You must attend work on time
- You must not leave your workstation without permission from your supervisor
- You must not smoke except in designated areas

These are examples of direct rules that identify proper conduct. Breaching the rules and engaging in misconduct should lead to disciplinary action. Serious or repetitive breaches should lead to dismissal, likely for cause.

The golden rule for rules is that you should be able to put each one on one page – two pages if you use pictures, diagrams and charts. If Moses was able to display the Ten Commandments on two stone tablets, you should be able to get workplace rules onto a page or two.

At the same time, remember that there were only Ten Commandments, and that was supposed to be the rulebook for life, not simply a workplace. I have seen many organizations make the mistake of trying to cram thirty disciplinary rules into a four-page foldout. Eyes will glaze over before your workers make it to the second page. Not even your supervisors will know anything after the tenth rule. If you really think that you need that many disciplinary rules, break them up into categories and post them separately. As with the third observation made above about procedures, "KISS" — keep it straightforward and simple. Use short words and short sentences. Use bullet points to replace paragraphs. Focus on the specific point that is the foundation for your rule.

Rules are not meant to trick your workers or to catch them on fine points. Your workers are meant to follow the rules. You want your workers to know about all of your rules and to understand them. It is therefore essential to communicate your rules so that they will be easily understood. If they are clear and well communicated, your rules can end up replacing the early stages of your progressive discipline system. There may be no need to give someone a verbal or even a written warning if you have a well established and widely communicated rule that identifies the standard that you require.

There are at least three important observations about procedures that would improve the operation of any workplace in terms of human resources management:

1. Procedures often constitute the detailed and concrete action plan for human resources policies. As such, from a practical standpoint, they are often incorporated into policies or appended to policies. From another direction, procedures can also be the specific articulation of longstanding practices, whether those practices relate to operational issues or aspects of human resources management. Understanding procedures in these contexts should assist in terms of overall consistency and design.

2. Procedures are meant to be read, and not simply by HRP's and management. Workers and their union representatives, as well as other categories of employees, are meant to read procedures. The beneficiaries or targets of the procedures have to read them. There should not be binders of procedures carefully locked away in the HRP's cabinets. Instead, there should be booklets distributed and posted that are easy to absorb. Revisions should be made on a periodic basis and updates should be re-distributed from time to time. If you have a booklet of policies and procedures, distribute it, make sure that your workers understand it is important, and re-distribute it every two or three years. Bear in mind that this is essentially what unionized organizations have to do with their collective agreements.

3. Many of your workers may not have graduated from high school, let alone have the benefit of post-secondary education. For many, English will not be their first language. Everyone, even university graduates, can better absorb short words, short sentences, short paragraphs and focused points. Use pictures, charts and diagrams. Use videos and photographs. Use internal websites and PowerPoint presentations. Remember that you are not trying to write a university paper, you are trying to communicate something that is important to the operation of your organization. Use all of the communication tools available to you. Whatever you do and however you do it, keep it straightforward and simple ("KISS").

Culture, History and Evolution

Workplaces can develop their own personalities. In modern society, each of us spends an incredible amount of time working and in the company of our work-mates. Nobody just punches in and out. Everybody does some living at work, although some are much more connected to workplace events and situations than is the case for others. Workplaces breed friendships, enemies and even intimate relationships, both inside and outside marriage. Many workers socialize with each other, while others avoid their co-workers outside the workplace and sometimes inside as well. This can be even more apparent with the presence of a union, as there is not only the workplace community for your workers, but there is also an overlapping trade union community.

In many workplaces, human resources managers and senior management typically turn over at a much faster rate than is the case for workers and front-line supervisors. In our fast-moving economy, it is normal to find private sector workplaces in which the workers and their union representatives have survived a number of ownership changes and even more changes in leadership. For new management and for all HRP's, it is absolutely imperative that you find out about the history of the workplace and that you get a sense of its personality or its culture before you try to stamp on a new identity.

The constant evolution of a workplace is inevitable, ongoing and often very beneficial, but the pace of change has to be carefully thought out and patiently managed. Rapid and abrupt change can be very disorienting for employees and damaging to a workplace, even if the ultimate direction of the change is positive. On the other hand, slow and deliberate change is probably entirely inappropriate in a crisis situation, where shock treatment may be much more in order.

The worst of all worlds, which happens more often than is sensible, is when the direction of a workplace swings back and forth with each leadership change, without any real regard for what has gone on over the long run and not simply in the latest incarnation of management. In those cases, either the workers will turn to their union for alternative leadership, or there will be a kind of underground leadership that develops. Employees may tune out management directives and revert to an unwritten way of doing things. Front-line supervisors may become similarly disillusioned. As a result, they may consciously, or through inactivity, work in league with the rebellious workers or even the union without much regard for the policies, procedures and rules that new management is trying to impose on the workplace.

A unionized workplace should be relatively stable by its very nature. Because of the collective agreement and the ongoing checks and balances provided by the presence of the union as a watchdog, there is generally a well-developed framework for the management of human resources. Problems can arise when the union creates unrealistic expectations among its members or when upper management has standards that are unreasonably high or that they want achieved too quickly. Problems can also arise when supervisors are at odds with management in terms of the ongoing operation of the workplace. Uncertainty, conflict and leaders who are out of touch with their people all combine to create a fertile climate for labour strife, both during the administration of the collective agreement and at the negotiating table.

Change in a workplace is inevitable and desirable, but it should be managed as much as possible. It should become part of the workplace culture. Workers and supervisors should be an integral part of change — they should see themselves as the architects of change and not simply its victims or its opponents. When we talk of having workers "buy-in" to change, we do not simply mean that management should be convincing as to the reasons for imposing change. Much better, we should look to the workers to participate in change and to convince themselves why the particular aspects of change are, at best, beneficial and, at worst, neutral to their own well-being in the workplace.

Unions are generally conservative by nature. They tend to resist change and even fear it. To a large degree, this caution is entirely understandable. For one thing, change has often been bad for unions and their members, at least in the short term. It has often meant technological innovations, reorganizations and even relocations. Quite typically, this has meant lost jobs, at least at the particular location where the union has bargaining rights.

For another thing, change is often badly handled by management at a unionized plant. The union often receives change as a "done deal" and has no opportunity to participate in planning for change or even to alert their members to the fact that change is imminent. Indeed, in many cases, the union will find out about the change at the same time as their members or even afterwards. That makes it a little difficult for union representatives to provide thought-out answers to the questions that members will naturally have to ask.

In my view, employers should always look for opportunities to get input from the union before implementing change. Management has the final say. There is no shared decision-making. That said, there is plenty of scope for harvesting ideas. The best ideas may come from the people who will be most directly impacted. At the very least, even without input, the union should always be informed of the change before their members, even if the advance notification is simply a matter of hours. If management fails to provide advance notification, it is simply asking for a fight.

◆
CHAPTER 3

GOOD HUMAN RESOURCES MANAGEMENT AT WORK

To this point, we have introduced the importance of good human resources management, along with the players in the workplace, as well as the legal and other boundaries that dictate the territory in which a Canadian workplace operates. It is time to put these people and these concepts to work. There are five building blocks that we will use on the path to good human resources management:

- Creating a framework
- Communicating expectations
- Correcting, cajoling and compliments — enforcing standards
- Complaints — creating an open atmosphere for questions and criticism
- Continuous renewal and inevitable change

The Framework

Each of these building blocks will be explored in a separate section, but before we get there, it is useful to look at the big picture. The overall goal is to produce goods or to provide services in an efficient and effective manner. Management's operational objectives are to minimize waste and maximize profitability (in the private sector) or relevance and usefulness (in the public sector).

We need people to achieve our objectives. We have already seen that people work for us or with us in many different guises. Our principal focus is on those who work for us as employees and, in particular, those who are workers, or subordinate employees. In a unionized workplace, these workers are the ones who form one or more bargaining units or potential units.

As soon as we have people working for us, a significant set of legal concepts springs into play. We have to operate our business or institutional activity subject to the limitations and costs created by these concepts. As a result, we want to understand and shape the concepts in the manner that makes it easiest for us to achieve our goals without undue restriction. Even with one or more unions present at the workplace, we should strive to maintain flexibility and control in managing all of our human resources.

The framework that we create, especially in terms of the collective agreement and the other self-imposed boundaries, should absorb the common law and legal requirements that face us. The law will compel certain aspects of the framework. Other aspects will be what we negotiate with the union and what we choose to include — the self-imposed boundaries. We want to achieve a seamless framework, so that there will be little, if any, visible distinction between that which we must do, that which we agree to do and that which we choose to do in respect of our employees, as we continue the pursuit of our business or institutional objectives.

Communication

The elements of the human resources framework, as well as our organizational objectives, must be communicated to our employees in a manner that is simple, straightforward and repetitive. We have to work towards a collective agreement that is, ideally, short, simply drafted and well organized. We have to post notices and identify key concepts and expectations. We have to distribute policy booklets that are written for the eyes of our employees and not for the back of a locked cabinet. We have to train on an ongoing and systematic basis.

Communication is a two-way street. An important avenue of communication is the complaint procedure (the grievance and arbitration procedure), which merits separate discussion below. The communication that draws our attention here is from the employer to its employees. What are you trying to achieve? How are you trying to achieve it? What are the standards of performance that you expect of your employees, both in terms of quality, quantity, and appropriate conduct?

For the most part and perhaps for all things, excellence is an entirely appropriate standard. You do not have to settle for mere adequacy. It is not enough, however, to want to be excellent. You have to be able to define excellence, to teach it, and to enforce it. Excellence is not a pipe dream; it is hard work. It requires both leadership, in terms of defining a vision and setting targets, and management, in terms of working with employees and their union representatives on a day-to-day basis to do the little things right so that, to a large extent, the big things will happen as an inevitable result.

Excellence also requires the willingness of management to stay principled when dealing with big things such as arbitrations and collective bargaining. Arbitrations often do not make sense on a straight dollars-and-cents basis. Similarly, some of the provisions that seem to take the longest to negotiate are the ones that make the least difference to bottom-line productivity and efficiency. Human resources management does not submit easily to a cost-benefit analysis, especially in a unionized workplace.

If you are forever settling grievances on a nuisance basis, what message are you communicating to the employees and their union? What the other side is hearing is, "management does not care to listen to our underlying issues and we might as well grieve even the silly stuff, because there is a good chance that we will get a pay-off".

The situation is similar at the bargaining table. Unless management is prepared to spend the time going through all issues that are tabled and making the effort to negotiate on the basis of principles and not expediency, then the union and the resulting collective agreement will end up out of control.

Agreements are built layer by layer, with each round of negotiations providing the basis for the next round, and all rounds afterwards. Management is responsible at each round to build a solid layer. Because the collective agreement acts as a restriction on management rights, a solid layer from the perspective of management should be not only thin, but it should have few if any innovations. In other words, it takes hard work and a commitment to excellence to achieve and maintain a collective agreement that restricts your management rights as little as possible. If you do so, in terms of taking care of this "big thing" called collective bargaining, your communication to your workers and their union is that you are serious about listening to their legitimate concerns and aspirations, but you are also committed to maintaining productive control of your workplace.

Performance Management

Most of our employees will "get it", almost all of the time. These are the employees who I refer to as able and willing. Some of our employees will resist or refuse or simply lack the motivation to achieve at the levels that we require; these are the ones who are able but unwilling. The employees who are able and willing deserve positive reinforcement. When these employees slip up, management has to react, but in a restrained manner that is designed to correct the sub-standard behaviour without creating undue resentment and antagonism. As we will discuss at greater length, significant misconduct requires a more significant response. In extreme cases, a single incident may be sufficient to fracture the employment relationship irreparably. As well, employees who are able but unwilling and who resist or refuse on an ongoing basis, even if each incident is relatively minor, may run out of chances to meet the reasonable standards that are set by management.

Beyond performance issues caused by employee misconduct or neglect, some employees may not "get it", or not often enough, because they may lack the qualifications, training, or intelligence to perform the work at the level that is expected. These are the employees who are willing but unable. Assuming that the established level of performance is achievable, and is being achieved, by other employees, then a management response is required, but it is not suitable to respond in a disciplinary fashion. As we will discuss, there are a range of non-disciplinary responses that are designed to assist these kinds of poor performers, up to and including non-disciplinary demotions or dismissals if required.

There is another kind of performance issue that exists, in addition to bad behaviour and inadequacy. That is the issue created by absenteeism. There are two main branches of the absenteeism problem. One branch is blameless absenteeism, which sometimes means that management cannot prove that the employee was absent without good reason. The other branch is culpable absenteeism, which features elements of misconduct, such as no-calls, no shows and late arrivals. Sometimes the two branches intertwine, such that the employee is off for a valid reason, but has not called in or communicated with management in the appropriate fashion.

The first branch — blameless absenteeism — has two sub-branches. The first of these is inhabited by unfortunate employees who have long-term debilitating illnesses or injuries, including disabilities that may prevent them from ever returning to their previous position, or to any kind of work. The second sub-branch generally requires more action from management. Here dwell the employees who have repetitive short-term absences, often for a variety of alleged ailments, some of which may be claimed as arising from workplace situations. Disciplinary action is not appropriate for blameless absenteeism, but there are non-disciplinary measures that management has at its disposal, and these often can be used to great effect to improve overall attendance.

For the most part, dealing with poor performance and poor attendance are significant management concerns, whether the cause is bad behaviour by the employee or bad luck. Employers should be careful in negotiating provisions in a collective agreement that deal with either performance or attendance, as those provisions generally act to restrict management rights. Management does not need permission from the collective agreement in order to deal with these workplace issues. Where the union will surely become involved, even if there are no collective agreement restrictions on management, is in reaction to discipline or attendance management consequences imposed on individual employees. Enforcing standards and dealing with employee complaints are issues that will be examined in more depth in Chapters 7 and 8 below.

Complaints

Many supervisors or managers like to boast about an open-door policy. In some cases, that is delusional thinking. In other cases, it is simply inadequate. One of the key aspects of a collective agreement, which is required by law, is a formal complaints procedure, called the grievance and arbitration procedure. Arbitration is the system of final and binding third-party adjudication that has replaced wildcat walkouts and strikes as the way in which workplace disputes are resolved while a collective agreement is in effect. Because of the system of arbitration, the only time that unionized employees can lawfully withdraw their services is at the end of an unsuccessful round of collective bargaining. The downside for employers is that many issues end up at arbitration that never would have motivated workers to engage in a wildcat walkout or strike.

Even with the cost and inconvenience to management of the grievance and arbitration system, it is tremendously important to ensure that employees have an effective outlet for complaints. It really does not matter whether or not the complaints are valid. What matters is that the employees have an opportunity to vent, and that management has a wide-open window onto whatever it is that is irritating the workers or any one of them.

In a unionized workplace, the key is to try to deal with complaints as early as possible. The last thing that management should want to see is their workers turning to their union, primarily because they feel that management is not listening to them or because their front-line supervisors lack the authority or are ineffective at resolving issues at the "shop-floor" or "office work station" level. Workplaces that feature insecurity, poor communication and perceived favouritism will likely become adversarial, overly legal, and consequently difficult to manage, even if the compensation package is reasonably good. If you want to see the union as little as possible, then a good place to start is by resolving complaints as quickly and effectively as possible.

Management cannot find out where it is perceived by its workers to be unfair and ineffective unless it is prepared to listen. You have to work at listening. It is not enough to say that you are willing to listen; you have to make it easy for employees to speak out. That requires both a culture of receptive listening and an effective complaint procedure with a focus on early resolution.

Renewal and Change

Nothing stays the same. Nothing lasts forever. Each of us is in a permanent state of change. Together, we are all changing, always. The only thing that you can count on is that you cannot count on anything.

To some extent, you can manage change. To other extents, you simply have to be ready to respond to change. To put this second point into clearer focus, think of any workday over the past few weeks or months. I challenge you to find even a single day when you went into work at the expected time, with a plan for the day, then achieved each part of your plan at the expected time and went home, happy and complete, at a reasonably normal quitting time.

This kind of pre-planned order rarely happens, if ever. Problems pop up all over the place, and often from entirely unexpected directions. Indeed, with e-mail and voice-mail, many of us now spend the first few minutes of each workday identifying all the surprises that combine to throw off our plan for the day before we have had even our first sip of coffee, tea or juice.

The last thing that I would ever tell you is "don't plan". On the contrary, planning is fundamental to the kind of leadership that I espouse. What I will tell you is that you should always keep room for the unexpected when you are making your plans. You should get away from the habit of saying that your day was thrown completely off balance by some unexpected event. That is a normal day. Instead, you should say that, as expected, you had to spend part of your day dealing with the unexpected.

In terms of your ability to manage change, I preach a calendar system, which is reviewed in further detail in section 9(b) below. For your key areas of human resources policy, like safety, human rights, productivity, technology and absenteeism, pick a month. September, a month of renewed focus, may be safety month. April, when everything is new again, may be human rights month. For most of you, do not bother with the summer months, because too many people are away at any given time, and always avoid the month that is your fiscal year end. That still leaves you with nine months to work with. Safety and human rights are requisite for every workplace — indeed, you may split human rights in two — discrimination and harassment. That will leave you with six or seven months for other areas that you consider to be key to your workplace.

Remember that, even in a unionized workplace, policy formulation, as well as the development of rules, procedures and practices, is almost entirely a management initiative. While I encourage employers to seek input from the workers and their union, management drives the process and makes the final decisions about the framework. Provisions in the collective agreement may restrict policy development, but the responsibility for workplace policies is firmly within the realm of management rights.

If you use the calendar system that I espouse, whatever month you choose for whatever policy should become enshrined for the indefinite future. For example, every September would be safety month. Every September, you will review and revise your safety policies and procedures. Every September, you will train your employees and run a communication campaign that features safety issues. That does not mean that you will ignore safety for the rest of the year. With an active safety committee, that would not be possible, and it is not desirable in any event.

What the calendar system ensures is that, whatever else may happen, for at least one month each year, there will be a particular focus on your key areas of human resources policy, such as safety. This will help the organization stay current and avoid the problems faced by many other organizations, when they do not realize how badly out-of-date they are until some serious situation arises. By then, it may be already too late.

◆

CHAPTER 4

CREATING A FRAMEWORK

So far, we have looked at the big picture. In the course of painting the big picture, many key details have become apparent. As we move into each of the specific areas of good human resources management in a unionized workplace, the intention is to zero in on many more specific issues and recommendations. In law and other areas of human endeavour, we often draw the distinction between the forest and the trees. To a great extent, thus far, I have been describing the forest. It is very important to keep the forest, the big picture, always in mind. It is not enough, however, to look only at the big picture. Just as you cannot sit in your office and expect to be effective in managing your people who are engaged in production or providing services, so too you cannot be satisfied with a general knowledge of the forest. You have to get right into it. You have to examine the individual trees and make your own assessment of what is rotten and what is sound. So, off we go, into the woods.

When we go into the woods, it is helpful to know where we are going, what we want to do on the way and once we get there, and how we get back out again. We need a set of objectives. We need to achieve some success quickly to reinforce the positive aspects of the journey. We need direction, both to get to where we want to go and to get back out again.

For the most part, we do not want to start from scratch. We want to find out the extent to which we already have useful elements of the framework. To know just how useful, and to help us identify what is missing, we should look to others who have gone into the same woods or who are in the process of making the same journey. Once we have taken an inventory and measured it, then we are in a position to complete our preparations for the trip.

So, to achieve a framework for good human resources management, the first step is to look at the policies, procedures, rules, practices, culture and history of our organization. We need to engage in a self-audit. We need to perform due diligence on our own organization, as if it were an organization that we might want to acquire and not simply the organization that we already have.

The second step is to look at other organizations that might provide for a useful comparison. This would include related or affiliated plants or offices, organizations within our geographical community or organizations within our industry or area of endeavour. For a non-union organization, it is very useful to find union counterparts. Having identified different comparators, we want to measure ourselves. Do they have pieces that are missing from our organization? Are there other pieces that they have in a different form that might improve on what we currently have? Do we have pieces that they do not have and we do not need, at least not to the extent of the current form?

The third step is to improve our framework — organize, modify, add, subtract, and organize again.

What Currently Exists

Every workplace at any stage in its existence, with the possible exception of the very beginning, already has two major repositories of knowledge: paper and people. Let us look at each of those.

There is paper everywhere in a workplace. If as much time was spent reading existing paper as is spent creating new paper, there might be much less paper. For purposes of human resources management, paper comes in two principal varieties. There is the general paper that is meant for the entire workplace — the policies, procedures, rules, notices, lists, health and safety minutes, blank forms and employee booklets (benefits, pensions, orientation and perhaps even phantom agreements in some form or other). There is also the personal paper that lives in the personnel files and medical files (if separate) that should exist for each employee.

There are three exercises that I find very useful in doing a paper audit of a unionized workplace. First, look in our offices and on our bulletin boards. Let us see what we find, in our desks and on our shelves. Is it consistent from supervisor to supervisor? Is it dated? Is it current? Do employees know it? Do they have a copy and, if not, why not? Do we have a distribution list to tell us who got what document and when it was received? Do we know what training we have provided and who was in attendance? What do we have posted and who is responsible for ensuring that required postings are current and in place?

The second exercise is to look at the records that are specifically related to our relationship with the trade union. Do we have negotiation files for previous rounds of collective bargaining? Do we have position descriptions and job evaluations? What about ergonomic assessments? Do we maintain tidy and consistent grievance files? Have we organized and kept copies of past arbitration decisions and settlements? Do we have files that cover other kinds of legal proceedings related to our people, including labour board, workers' compensation, health and safety and human rights cases?

The third exercise is to look in the personnel files. Are the files tidy? Are the documents on some sort of a brad so that they are not loose? Are they in reverse chronological order? Are there meaningful separations, so that medical information is kept apart from other information? Is discipline kept separate and is it in keeping with any collective agreement restrictions? Are there performance evaluations and, if so, are they regular or haphazard? Do employees have access to their files and would we be prepared to show them what we have?

It is not enough for you to bury yourself in paper. You also have to get to know your people. Part of the HRP's job is to get out to where the workers are on a regular, daily basis. This is even more necessary for supervisors. You need to identify your long-service workers, the natural leaders, the over-achievers and the outsiders. Who are your problem employees, whether in terms of discipline, poor attendance or low skill?

At a higher level, you need to identify how your supervisors are performing, both as a group and on an individual basis. Are they on side? Do they have confidence and the necessary will to administer discipline, enforce standards, and follow the policies, procedures and rules of your workplace? Do they feel empowered or do they fret about a history of perceived and possibly real betrayal by higher levels of management? Are they working with reasonable consistency as a team or are there hard supervisors and soft ones, sowing confusion among the workers and decreasing respect for the management team as a whole? Is the supervisory workload fairly distributed? Do your supervisors play it strictly by the book or do they understand the meaning of discretion and do they exercise reasonable judgement at appropriate times? Do they have an even keel or are they emotional and possibly biased in dealing with their subordinate workers?

Who are the union leaders, both inside and outside the workplace? What relationship lines exist between management and the union representatives? With a good relationship, the union can stay out of your way and even be helpful in some situations. With an adversarial relationship, you may waste a tremendous amount of time and energy in dealing with grievances and legal proceedings.

You will not get to know your people overnight. You will also not get to know them by accident. You have to make the effort to meet with your people one-on-one and in groups. You should have a plan for meeting your people and you should set deadlines. When you meet, you have to overcome the tendency to talk to your people and learn to get them to talk to you. The more listening you can do, the more you will learn. This is not a one-off exercise; it is continuous. Once you have met with your people, you have to start to meet them all over again.

Other Models

All organizations have a number of other organizations to which they can compare. In most cases, it is pretty easy to get decent information about how those other organizations manage their human resources. In making such comparisons, you have two complementary objectives. First, you want to organize your own workplace in an effective manner, and you want to offer reasonable and relevant terms and conditions to your workers. Second, you want to minimize the impact of the collective agreement and the union on the management of human resources at your plant.

Here is what you are looking for:

- Other collective agreements, especially with the same union and local.
- Arbitration decisions and possibly labour relations board decisions.
- In either union or non-union workplaces, wrongful dismissal decisions, and decisions of administrative tribunals dealing with matters of human rights, employment standards, health and safety and workers' compensation; with co-operation from other workplaces, you might also have access to settlements.
- Written policies, especially those dealing with human rights issues and safety.
- Employee handbooks and employee orientation manuals.
- Benefits and pension handbooks.
- Wage schedules.

- Procedures, especially complaint procedures, scheduling of work and overtime, attendance management, leave procedures and scheduling vacations.
- Rules, especially setting out disciplinary infractions and safety rules.

Here are some places to look:

- Look at other plants or offices within your own company or organizational structure; or look within associated or related organizations. These are your own people. Perhaps you already receive significant information from them. If not, it should be easy to get information, especially in these days of enhanced electronic transfer of data.
- Look within your community, especially if you are in a smaller town. Smaller communities typically feature a handful of significant industries or public sector employers (such as hospitals, or municipal or county government). The questions to ask yourself are: for whom do my employees' children, parents and spouses work? For whom would my employees work if not with us? Answer those questions and you will know whom to contact for information. Note that information about unionized operations is always pretty easy to get. Collective agreements are not private contracts; they are public documents that are accessible to anyone who wants to take a look. As well, there may be decisions — especially arbitration decisions — that are easy to access. In any event, HRP's are usually quite helpful to each other, as you should be to other HRP's. You can often get as much information as you could reasonably handle, simply by asking for it.
- Be alert to where relatives or friends of your employees are employed. The next set of issues that become featured during collective bargaining may be imported from some other workplace — sometimes by the union, but sometimes by your own workers based on what their friends and relatives are getting.
- Look within your industry, wherever your competitors, suppliers or customers may be located. If you supply product to a unionized company or if a unionized company supplies you, you can expect that your employees will point to the terms and conditions in place at your key unionized customers

and suppliers if there is an argument that they are superior to what is in place at your own plant. At the same time, the companies in your own industry provide an excellent resource for terms and conditions that would be suitable with your employees.

Creating Your New or Improved Framework

Start with the big picture, and then get into the details. Make sure that you give yourself some early successes. You do not have to achieve everything at once. You should not expect that what you achieve is going to last forever. Try to head in a generally consistent direction, and avoid swinging about like a weather vane in shifting winds. Expect to review and revise whatever you achieve on an ongoing basis, but try to maintain your overall direction. Success is achieved step by step, in small increments. Here are some steps you can take in a sequence that makes sense, but is obviously subject to your own current situation and requirements:

1. Separate your employees into groups, such as blue-collar, white-collar, front-line supervisors, middle managers and professionals, and senior executives. The existence of one or more bargaining units will make this separation pretty straightforward. Some aspects of human resources management will apply to all groups; other aspects will apply uniquely or differently to individual groups. Once you have different groups identified, you will be able to divide your employees further into sub-groups such that, for your workers in particular, you will be able to identify an existing classification structure.
2. Establish or review and revise your principal policies, such as human rights, safety, attendance management, modified work, confidential employee assistance and job evaluation.
3. Establish or review and revise your principal terms and conditions of employment, which will be largely set out in your collective agreement(s):
   - hours of work, including scheduling and breaks;
   - relevance of service and seniority to promotions and lay-offs
   - leaves of absence, including pregnancy leave, parental leave, emergency leave and bereavement leave;
   - vacation entitlement and holidays;

- wages, including premium pay and overtime;
- benefits and pension entitlement;
- perquisites, including paid uniforms and safety equipment (such as footwear and eyeglasses).

4. Establish or review and revise such major procedures as discipline, non-disciplinary warnings for attendance problems, and a procedure for employee complaints at the outset of the grievance procedure.

5. Establish or review and revise such other procedures as:
   - bringing human rights concerns to the attention of management and how such concerns will be investigated;
   - how safety incidents are to be reported and investigated;
   - how workplace accidents or illnesses thought to be caused by the workplace are to be reported and investigated;
   - how employees are to return to work following illnesses or injuries — including work trials and work hardening periods;
   - dealing with employees who have drug or alcohol abuse issues and circumstances under which the employer will support rehabilitation programs, including funding;
   - how employees who are absent, late, or who want to leave early or for part of the work day are supposed to communicate such absences or requests for short leave to the employer;
   - dealing with employees who are incarcerated — whether or not the employer will participate in temporary absence programs and circumstances under which leaves of absence will be granted;
   - how jobs will be evaluated in the event of changes in procedures or equipment; you will want to consider whether or not you have job descriptions; in a manufacturing operation or other operation requiring physical labour, these in turn may be based on physical demands analyses, ergonomic reports, or other work environment reviews;
   - how job vacancies will be posted and how employees go about bidding for such vacancies;
   - how work will be scheduled and, if there are shifts, whether or not employees will be able to switch shifts with other employees, and how they do that;
   - how overtime will be scheduled or assigned and which employees have access to the overtime work;

- how employees apply for leaves of absence, including emergency leave;
- whether or not there will be lieu days or floating holidays that need to be scheduled, and how employees are supposed to do that;
- how employees apply for benefits; and
- how employees apply for such perquisites as safety footwear and safety glasses.

Note that many of the above procedures may be restricted by the collective agreement or affected to some extent by provisions in the collective agreement; however, to a significant degree, these procedures will be within the control of management and may be revised without having to be negotiated.

6. Establish or review and revise any specific rules that are particular to your operation. Rule-making is a basic management right, subject only to specific restrictions in the collective agreement. Here are some points to remember:
   - if your rules are not on one page, get busy editing or re-organizing your rules;
   - break your rules into more bite-size pieces;
   - add some graphics;
   - make sure that there is a consequence clearly identified for breaching a rule;
   - never paint yourself into a corner; no consequence should be automatic; you should not force yourself to manage simply "by the book" – management should always retain a discretion to act in a manner that best fits the particular circumstances of any situation; each case is potentially different from every other case.

7. Make sure that you are left with a co-ordinated and cohesive set of materials. Think of your framework as a desktop. You do not want a jumble of paper and files and stuff piled in a haphazard mess that makes sense to nobody else, and possibly not even to you. Instead, you want a tidy desk that someone replacing you could sit behind for the first time and, with a reasonable period of familiarization, your replacement could start to function in a manner consistent with everything that had gone on before.

This tidy desk should be more than an analogy. It should be, in effect, your objective as you create your framework. Whether analogy or reality, here is what your replacement might find on your tidy desk:

- right in the middle of the desk would be the collective agreement; your agreement should be rumpled and marked up to show that it is well read and well used;
- right beside the collective agreement would be a binder of policies, neatly tabbed and indexed, with procedures and forms appended to each policy; the procedures and forms would be created in a manner intended for general distribution and use by workers and other employees;
- off to one side would be a booklet for distribution to employees setting out some or all of the following: benefits, pension (if applicable), vacation entitlement, holidays, leave entitlement, perquisites, classifications and a wage structure; some of these may be covered in the collective agreement, but many of these require additional details or a simplified explanation, which is perfectly acceptable so long as the collective agreement is not contradicted;
- on the other side would be a set of rules designed for posting in your workplace;
- in your desk drawer would be pads with disciplinary reports, incident reports, job vacancy postings and applications, leave applications, and vacation request forms; the union will provide the grievance forms; some operations may also require time sheets and overtime sheets if this is not handled separately by a payroll group;
- in another desk drawer would be any form that may be required for government filings, such as workers' compensation forms and records of employment.

Creating Buy-In with Your Management Team, Your Workers and the Union(s)

In developing policies, procedures, booklets, rules and forms, and in lining up workplace practices with all of this activity, you should actively seek buy-in throughout the process. To a large extent, this will be a top-down process. Developing booklets and forms is not generally a group activity and somebody has to initiate and drive the process of creating the framework. There remains plenty of opportunity for input, there is a tremendous need for communication and training, and there should be an ongoing process of framework development and renewal. In looking for buy-in, you should have at least three objectives to keep in mind with your management team, your workers and their union representatives, and other employees:

1. You want their widespread input before finalizing any policies, procedures and rules because the other players in your workplace might have very good ideas. You never start with a blank slate and there are different stages for gathering input. Presumably you are acting at the outset with a mandate from senior management and with the active participation of at least some of the members of the management team. Once you have a cohesive draft, you could then seek input from the entire management team, front-line supervisors in particular. Once you have a completed draft, but prior to implementation, you should consider seeking input from your workers and their union representatives, and other employees. For this purpose, you could have the non-union employees appoint their own representatives, either on an ongoing basis or for the purposes of this project. Alternatively, you could make the selections yourself, so that you achieve a representative sampling of the employee population.

2. As well as producing good ideas that will improve your framework, input also creates widespread ownership. If only for this purpose, you should actively seek out opportunities to implement some of the suggestions you receive, especially those from the representatives of workers and other employees. A classic negotiating tactic is to give the other side options for settlement. This quite often ends with them debating over which of your options they are prepared to accept, whereas they might have opposed each option if presented separately. In the same way, when developing policies, procedures and rules, you should consider providing your target audiences with alternatives. As soon as they start serious consideration of your alternatives, they will have accepted the framework itself – the rest is simply detail.

In the ancient civilized world, it used to be said that all roads lead to Rome. My own translation of that, using our analogy of travelling into the forest, is that there are many paths to the clearing in the middle of the forest that is our destination. Your objective is not so much to dictate the path that has to be travelled. Instead, your principal objective is to get everyone headed in the same general direction towards the same destination. If they want to choose their path, especially if it is one of the paths that you suggested in the first place, then they are all the more likely to ensure that the path they have chosen is a good route.

3. Once you have your framework in place, at least in part, you have to promote it actively. As a lesson in what not to do, let us consider a common experience in a unionized workplace. Two negotiating committees work hard to achieve a collective agreement. As is typical, they go through conciliation and are facing the prospect of a work stoppage before a settlement if finally achieved. Then there is a nervous period of a few days while the negotiators wait for completion of the ratification process. Finally, after a close vote, the workers approve the settlement. Then, nothing much happens, other than implementing the increases in the compensation package. It takes forever to produce the new collective agreement. There is no training of front-line supervisors and other members of the management team as to the significant changes in the terms and conditions of employment. Indeed, there is no overall review of the agreement itself.

Try to avoid this dead zone after the achievement of a collective agreement. Get in there. Be prompt and thorough. Promote common understanding between workers and management. Create trust with the union. Promote consistency within your management team. Make sure that everyone understands his or her role. Make sure that your front-line supervisors understand the authority that they have and its limits. Promote the supporting role of the HRP and make it clear that the management of human resources primarily lies with those who are responsible for operational management.

If you do a good job securing buy-in, then you will be well on the way to communicating your expectations, both to the management team and to the rest of the workforce.

Gaining Input while Maintaining Control

Input is important. Buy-in at different levels is important in developing an effective framework. In securing input and creating buy-in, HRP's should focus continuously on three key points:

1. Although many may participate, someone, or a small group of people, has to drive the process. It is up to the HRP to create or directly oversee the preparation of the initial draft of any documents that are part of the framework. The HRP must oversee revisions and ensure that any input receives a prompt response. The HRP must set an overall timeframe, with interim targets; otherwise, projects will suffer the fate of so many good intentions and trail off into nothing.

2. I strongly encourage seeking input from the union. This does not mean that the union shares responsibility for management of the workplace. The union is a participant and sometimes an adversary. The leader and the ultimate decision-maker is management. Final say should never be shared or given away.

3. Simply because input is received does not mean that it has to be implemented. Management must retain ultimate control. Management has the final say in respect of the framework. Input that is not consistent with management's vision cannot be incorporated into the framework.

   At the same time, if you are serious about input and you convince your employees that the input process is important, you will create expectations that should be met. The way to balance the need to maintain control with the importance of gaining input is to manage the input process. Here are some tactics:

   - rather than firing off draft documents and requesting feedback, focus the input; make the process "user-friendly"; take different segments of a policy or a procedure and ask employees to respond to specific questions;
   - as was discussed in section 5(d), provide employees with options, so that they are selecting between alternatives that already have been determined to be acceptable to management;
   - use discussion groups, which have the effect of gathering input and training the employees at the same time;
   - use questionnaires and surveys;

- avoid pride of authorship – if you receive a suggestion that is worded differently or framed differently, but seems just as effective, consider deferring to the input instead of the original draft;
- provide feedback to employees about the input received, including explanations as to why certain ideas have not been incorporated into the framework;
- thank employees for the input received, even if it is not used, and look for ways to give it value – for example, "even though your idea was not accepted, it caused us to think about this other aspect of the policy and to make the following additional changes";
- follow through – employees who take the time to make suggestions or to respond to inquiries do not necessarily expect that their views will be incorporated into the framework; however, they certainly expect something to happen.

Once you invite your employees and their union representatives to participate in the process of developing a framework, which includes the ongoing process of review and revision, do not abandon them. Management continues to be the ultimate decision-maker. As such, management has decided to involve employees in the process. Do not betray your own decision to create participation. If you open the door, only to ignore your invited guests, then you will find that you have pushed your employees further away than if you had not bothered to consult them in the first place. In trying to create a climate of co-operation, your failure to foster meaningful participation will create mistrust and adversity.

There are many ways to shape the input process and to demonstrate that you value the input received and, at the same time, to achieve the kind of framework that you consider to be consistent with operational objectives. Invite input. Look for ways to use it while retaining overall control of the policy and the process. Continue to invite input after implementation. Remain open to change before, during and after implementation.

◆
CHAPTER 5

COMMUNICATING EXPECTATIONS

Once you have established a basic framework, you have to be both skilled and diligent in communicating your expectations to the human resources who you intend to manage. Remember that management has the fundamental and central right to organize the workplace and to set and enforce the standards for performance and acceptable conduct, subject to the boundaries that we have discussed. Your framework provides a basic structure, but organizing a workplace and achieving standards is an ongoing activity. To avoid a communications breakdown, here are the groups that you have to focus on and how you should approach each group:

Higher Level Management

To support the effective management of an organization's human resources, higher-level management has to travel in two directions. In one direction, higher-level management has to be fully involved. In the other direction, they have to stay out of the way. Although these may seem to be contradictory tasks, they are harmoniously achieved at different levels and at different stages in the process.

We will start with staying out of the way. Front-line supervisors and the second-level managers to whom they directly report have day-to-day responsibility for human resources management. Higher-level management has to support that responsibility at every turn. I have seen operations where that lesson has been forgotten or never learned. The result is that workers ignore their immediate supervisors and, with the blind concurrence of senior management, the supervisors are effectively marginalized. If there are new practices to implement, the workers will confirm their validity with senior management. If there is corrective action to hand out or if performance is to be evaluated, it will be ignored or resisted unless and until senior management validates it. If there are complaints, even of a fairly trivial nature, they cannot be settled without the intervention of senior management.

This is very destructive to the management team. It is a waste of money and a waste of supervisory talent. It is a waste of senior management's time. But it is even worse than that. Front-line supervisors bad-mouth senior management, perhaps without always realizing what they are doing. If workers complain about policies, procedures, rules or new practices, supervisors might retort, "we are just doing what we are told" or "take it up with the management", seemingly in ignorance of the fact that they are or should be part of the management team. For their part, without sufficient hands-on knowledge of the day-to-day operations or the workers, senior management often make poor decisions that are designed more to avoid disputes than to support the framework of human resources management. Decisions that get the product out or keep up a high level of delivery of services in the short-run may be very damaging in the long-term, or perhaps much sooner than that.

Here is where it should be clear that any reference to HRP's as support staff is not intended to suggest, in any way, that HRP's are somehow minor players. By contrast, HRP's have to be strong, knowledgeable, committed, and more than a little stubborn. It is up to the HRP to ensure that supervisors feel that they are included in the management team and to ensure that all supervisors have bought-in to the program to the extent that they treat it as their own program. In such an environment, workers who have complaints will be met by supervisors who are eager to explain and support whatever part of the framework has generated the complaint. More important, such supervisors will be eager to resolve the complaint at the earliest possible opportunity and in the most effective manner possible.

It is also up to the HRP to ensure that senior management is fully informed and has the opportunity to be fully involved in the big picture. Senior management should, for the most part, be able to avoid the nuts and bolts of human resources management. In addition to the overall framework itself, senior management should be involved only in particularly serious situations or if a complaint cannot be resolved at an early level.

Indeed, in this respect, the most important understanding that the HRP can forge with senior management is the extent to which they are prepared to delegate authority to front-line and/or second-line supervisors. This is especially true in terms of disciplinary authority, but stretches to all areas where management has discretionary decision-making power. It is unhealthy to give away all authority but, within limits, supervisors should be given as much autonomy and as much decision-making authority as they can reasonably handle.

Front-Line Supervisors

Front-line supervisors fulfil a key function in the management of any workplace. The responsibility for effective human resources management falls most directly on their shoulders. The success of the policies of management — whether for work production, safety or employee relations — will, to a large extent, be determined by the day-to-day actions of your supervisors. In some situations, the actions of an individual supervisor may have far-reaching implications for the whole organization. It is therefore an ongoing responsibility of HRP's and senior management to ensure that front-line supervisors have the training and support that are necessary for them to manage effectively. Supervisors who know what they are doing, and who trust the rest of the management team to back them up in their efforts, will have the tools necessary to be workplace leaders.

Here are the three biggest messages to deliver consistently to your supervisors:

- the supervisors must follow the framework, as individuals and collectively as a group – there should be plenty of opportunity for input when the framework is first established and when it is reviewed, modified and renewed thereafter, but in the meantime the framework should be respected; it is more than a mere guideline;
- consistency is key – each supervisor has to be consistent as an individual on a day-to-day basis; as well, the members of the management team have to be consistent with each other and supportive of each other;
- the decisions that supervisors make matter; and their decision-making authority, within limits, will be supported by senior management; however, both to maintain consistency and to promote harmony among the workers, supervisors have to understand that support for supervisors will be neither blind nor universal.

Following the Framework

The rules for following the framework are especially important for supervisors in a unionized workplace, who have to operate within the restrictions imposed by a collective agreement:

1. Be thoroughly familiar with the framework, including the collective agreement, and how it dovetails with labour and employment legislation and with the requirements and expectations of the employer:
   - get help from human resources, your colleagues or your boss if you do not understand the framework or the law;
   - give employees what they are entitled to receive;
   - do not expand the framework through loose or inconsistent application.

2. The framework decides what is "fair"; the framework is not subject to individual application either by a supervisor or towards workers; a supervisor should be neither a soft touch nor a taskmaster and should not create the perception or the reality of preferential treatment.

3. The framework, and the collective agreement in particular, is a limitation on management rights; you want to limit yourself as little as possible; therefore, interpret ambiguous or generally worded provisions in management's favour.

4. Know management's position on contentious issues or ambiguous provisions.

5. Management acts; the workers and their union representatives react; do not compromise your authority; do not share your responsibility for interpreting and applying the framework with your workers or the union(s).

6. Supervisors will have discretionary powers in many situations; supervisory discretion always should be exercised in a manner that is reasonable; it should not be arbitrary or discriminatory, and it should demonstrate good faith.

7. Ensure that your workers are notified promptly and clearly of any changes in the framework and any changes in practice that you are implementing.

8. Thoroughly review any decision or settlement in terms of its impact on the framework. In particular, if a grievance is settled or an arbitrator makes a determination, that settlement or decision will either reinforce or actually change the meaning of the collective agreement.

9. Consider your actions and justify your decisions within the context of the framework and operational requirements; always consider the impact that your actions or your application of the framework will have on the entire organization.

Consistency

Nothing destroys the framework faster than inconsistent application. Consistency is easy to preach, but not so easy to practise. Here are three key aspects:

1. Each supervisor has to be internally consistent. Nobody is a machine. There will always be workers who rub you the wrong way and other workers who are easy to assist even when they are not achieving your standards. You will have good days, better days, and days to forget. That is the beauty of a good framework. As part of the management team, you have helped to develop the policies, procedures and rules that will frame your day-to-day practices with little regard to whom you are dealing with and how you are feeling about it, or indeed how you are feeling in general. This is not so much managing by the book. Rather, it is managing on a solid and comprehensive foundation, with the limitations or boundaries clearly understood.

2. You have to avoid the reality and the perception of playing favourites. Applying behavioural standards should not vary depending on a worker's job performance in terms of quality and quantity. High performers can be directly rewarded for that, but they should have to meet the same standards of conduct as other workers. In the same way, employees who are models of good behaviour still have to meet the standards set for quality and quantity of output. Some workers can be like children, with antennae especially tuned to any kind of imbalance in treatment.

Do not let your enthusiasm for fairness carry you away. There are at least three common traps that you should avoid:

- Your goal is equitable treatment, not equal treatment. You are managing human beings, not solving mathematical problems. There are no perfect answers and there are no perfect systems of comparison between different people.
- Your focus should be on process, not results. Results will likely differ for different people in different circumstances. The framework, along with consistent practice, should provide both the appearance and the reality of equitable treatment in terms of your approach to different employees in similar situations.

- You should try to preserve the right to reward employees who exceed standards, just as you are obligated to assist employees who are falling short. Indeed, you may have a legal obligation to assist employees whose shortcomings are attributable, at least in part, to a disabling condition. That said, an employee who is disabled should be entitled to accommodation, but not preferential rights to a promotion without regard to the service or qualifications of other employees. One of your challenges in a unionized workplace will be to avoid or limit collective agreement restrictions on your right to reward high-achieving employees. Many employers are pushing for provisions like merit pay; incentive plans, including piecework; profit sharing; and promotions based on merit rather than seniority. The key, whether with rewards or assistance, is that there should be a direct link and, for the most part, the link should be broadcast in advance.

3. Each supervisor and each member of the management team has to strive to be consistent with every other member of the team. Naturally, there will be different styles and different strengths. Those differences are no excuse for ignoring the framework, making things up as you go along or simply failing to do what you should be doing in order to avoid conflict. The goal is relative consistency, not absolute equality of treatment between supervisors. Indeed, nobody has all the right answers and each supervisor can be both student and teacher at different times in interaction with the rest of the management team.

Here again the HRP has a key role to play. Understanding, observing and assessing the different supervisory styles is necessary to achieve and maintain a balanced approach to all of the people working in your operation. Some supervisors need to be toned down and others need to be pushed, prodded or pulled into more activity. Every supervisor I have ever met has benefitted from ongoing communication about the expectations of the organization, as well as regular training in human resources management.

The Workers

Communication with the workers occurs in at least five ways:

1. *Distribution of paper.* This has been discussed at length already in terms of the development of the framework. What is important to remember is that the paper is more important to the members of management who developed it than it is to the workers who are its recipients. You cannot assume that they will value the paper like you do. You have to create the value. You have to hammer away at its importance. You should get employees to sign for whatever is handed to them, and you should be clear as to your expectations about retention. If it is to be retained in the workplace, you should perform an occasional audit. If it can be retained at home, you may ask that it be brought in from time to time for your review. You should make retention easy, with solid covers or binders in which the paper can be safely stored. You have to be prepared to hand out replacement copies. You have to plan to hand out revisions on a regular basis, likely every two or three years. As part of your training, you should test employees on their knowledge of different aspects of the framework.

   The one set of paper that many workers will value and that they may even know better than you do is the collective agreement. No problem with that — the collective agreement collects many of the terms and conditions of employment and represents the extent to which management was prepared to limit its rights. As such, the employees should be entitled to the agreements represented by the provisions in the collective agreement.

2. *General communication and training.* Whether in one-off assemblies of the entire workforce or through formal training programs, you will likely deal with your workers on an operations-wide basis in respect of certain aspects of the framework.

3. *Work group communication and training.* However your workforce is organized, it will likely feature smaller groups that are led by a supervisor. Depending on the needs of your operations and on the closeness of supervision, these employees may meet together on a daily or weekly basis. At the very least opportunities

should be created on a regular basis every couple of weeks for the sharing of information.

4. *Individual and situational communication.* Through corrective action or performance evaluation, both informally and formally, on a regular basis or as needed, each individual worker will receive direct communication that relates to what that particular worker is doing.

5. *Informal communication — the rumour mill.* You cannot stop the rumour mill. You cannot effectively control what employees say to each other. What you have to do is to try to stay plugged in, set up your own network to counteract the negative impacts of the rumour mill, and react in a more formal way when the rumour mill threatens to get out of hand. Remember not to overreact. This is a natural part of any human gathering. Although rumours can be very harmful, they often can be relatively benign and allow your people to let off some steam.

The Union

You will communicate with the union because you have to, at collective bargaining and during the grievance and arbitration procedure. You should also communicate with the union because it makes sense to do so, in terms of gathering input as you develop and continuously revise the framework.

Within the workplace, you will deal with union stewards, as well as other elected or appointed representatives of the union. Except to the extent that the collective agreement allows union representatives to be paid in whole or in part for attending to union business, the rule is that union stewards must still perform their work at the quality and in the quantity that you expect of other employees. The challenge for management and the union alike is to have a relationship of relative equality when dealing with union matters while retaining a traditional relationship of supervisory authority in terms of the inside union representative's responsibilities as a worker.

The union will also have outside representation in terms of the business agent or equivalent, who is a full-time employee of the union with responsibility for your workplace, and usually many other workplaces as well. Most outside union representatives whom I have met become difficult to deal with because of one thing and that is the failure of management to let them know what is coming down the track before it hits them. With even a modest amount of experience, an outside union representative will get a pretty wide perspective — they will see lay-offs, terminations, closures, dishonesty on all sides and plenty of disappointment. They will see tough negotiations, lost votes, work stoppages, and some degree of violence and plenty of bad tempers. They will give and get tough talk and smooth talk. All of this they can handle. What they really hate is to be blind-sided. The payment for that will be long and large. My recommendation in dealing with a union business agent is, if possible, avoid surprises.

Other Workplace Players

For the purposes of this book, I have tried to maintain a distinction between workers and other workplace players, who are considered at some length in chapter 2. They include professionals, confidential employees and third parties. In large measure, that distinction is important because it marks out the targets for union organization.

Different groups should not lead to multiple frameworks. All workplace players, regardless of how they are grouped, should be subject to the same framework, at least in terms of the applicable parts, and most parts should be generally applicable. Even third parties need to know "the rules of the road", although they are not subject to any of the aspects of compensation that apply to employees, and they are not managed, disciplined or evaluated in a traditional way.

You will have to tailor your framework to the different sections of your audience, but the general rule is to apply as much of it to as many of the workplace players in as many situations as possible. To the extent that it is applied, it should be communicated at least that much and possibly more. There is rarely much harm in providing too much information. It is always a deficiency to provide not enough information or to provide the information, but not often enough.

Communication is a Two-way Street

Although most of our attention has been on communications from the management team to workers and other workplace players, most readers will be keenly aware that communication goes both ways. In chapter 5, we talked about the importance of input, both for the value of the information received and for the inherent value of creating buy-in to the framework. In chapter 8 we will look at a particular system of receiving information from employees through complaints and the grievance procedure. Beyond this, it is important for HRP's to reinforce continually with front-line supervisors and all members of the management team that there is no replacement to active listening to all workplace players. The first awareness of big problems may come from very quiet and minor suggestions or complaints from workers.

Here are some specific suggestions for active listening in the workplace:

- You have to be regularly available on the shop floor, in the office area, or on the road, where employees actually work; you have to be in the employee's normal work environment in order to hear what they are trying to communicate.
- Trust is difficult to acquire; it can be lost in a single incident. To be effective as a listener, you have to be trusted by your workers. If you are told something in confidence, the confidence must be respected. If law or policy means that you cannot maintain confidentiality (such as with an allegation of sexual harassment or unsafe work practices), then the employee must be advised, with an explanation, that you have overriding obligations as a supervisor.
- Language barriers or a lack of sophistication on the part of employees can garble the message, but should not diminish its importance; make a special effort to listen to employees who are difficult to understand.
- What you are actually told may not be the real problem. Active listening requires probing; use focused, open-ended questions to get to the bottom of the real issue.
- Sometimes the workers who irritate you the most are the ones to whom you have listened most closely.
- It is hard to listen when you are talking.
- Listen first, talk second; an employee may be uncomfortable making a suggestion or raising a concern when you have already made your point.
- Follow up. You may not get the full story the first time around.
- If you tell the employee or a union representative that you will follow up, make sure that you do so. Give the employee a time frame, and then be timely in your follow-up. If you need more time, make sure that you advise the employee or union representative of the delay.

◆

CHAPTER 6

ENFORCING STANDARDS

Having set standards and communicated your expectations to your people, you have to measure continuously whether or not your standards are being met. To a great extent, you will work with the entire group. Ultimately, what matters is the performance of the entire team. Remember that the team is made up of individuals. In certain areas, some of your individuals will perform above the standards that you have set, whether in terms of quality, quantity, or both. Excellence should be recognized and rewarded. This may be as simple as a "thank you" and "well done" or it may involve creative and sophisticated incentive or merit pay schemes. However you do it, you know, or you will find out, that standards are subject to being enforced with the carrot as well as with the stick.

Unfortunately, whatever you do, some individuals will fail to meet your standards at least some of the time. If this is happening often, with many of your employees, then there may be a problem with your standards, your communication, or the skills and qualifications of your workers. If this is happening with some of your employees, but not with most others, then the problem is with the individual employee. The problem may be a disciplinary problem, in that the employee is failing to work at the level of his/her skill and ability. Or, the problem may be non-disciplinary, in that the employee wants to meet your standards, but is simply incapable of doing so.

We will look at four different ways of enforcing standards. Performance evaluations and merit pay each will receive a relatively brief mention. Most of our attention will be on a disciplinary system that I call the corrective action plan, with some time spent at the end on the distinct issue of non-disciplinary action.

Performance Evaluations

Performance evaluations are usually a pain and rarely done well. Used properly, evaluations can be a very effective management tool. Here are eight suggestions:

1. *Probationary Employees.* Employers should apply probationary periods in most cases, although it may not be appropriate for senior or exceptionally qualified employees. Probationary periods

are typically featured in collective agreements and generally allow for the dismissal of an employee without just cause. In any case, a probationary employee should never be dismissed in an unreasonable or arbitrary manner. To provide a justifiable basis for evaluating new employees, it should be a standard requirement that performance evaluations be done as part of any probationary period. In some cases, evaluations might be done every few weeks, in accordance with a pre-set schedule.

It is bad enough that some employers do not take advantage of probationary periods at all. Worse still are those who have a probationary period, but fail to evaluate new employees properly. It is a sad case when a negative evaluation is completed after the probationary period has finished – sometimes only by a matter of days or weeks, but still too late as a matter of application of the collective agreement. In other cases, there is no evaluation and yet a determination is made some time after the probationary period that the employee is unsatisfactory. In a unionized environment, it is very difficult to dismiss an employee for performance once s/he has attained seniority standing.

In some cases, employees are dismissed before the probationary period has expired, but without the benefit of a proper evaluation. That is the kind of arbitrary and unreasonable decision-making that leads to grievances based on allegations of bad faith or even discrimination. It is simply inadequate from the standpoint of human resources management and should be avoided. There is a saying that bad facts make bad law. I have seen probationary provisions that have been respected for years come under challenge simply because the employer was not reasonable or sensible in dealing with a particular employee and the union was left with little choice but to challenge the legality of the probationary clause.

2. For employees who have passed the probationary period, evaluations should be done on an annual basis. The employer should pick the same time period each year, somewhat in advance of a decision about compensation increases, which also should be determined at the same time for all employees in most cases. It is up to the HRP to monitor the process and to ensure that evaluations are completed. The support of senior management is obviously very helpful. The collective agreement rarely restricts the right to evaluate performance.

3. Technology can be usefully applied to ease the burden of completing performance evaluations. Some organizations are now completing evaluations using an internal web form.

4. Employees should be required to complete a self-evaluation in advance of the supervisor's evaluation. This can be a very effective tool that can also ease the burden of the evaluation.

5. The evaluation should look forward as well as backward. Goals should be set and part of the following year's evaluation should be based on the extent to which the previous year's goals were achieved.

6. Performance evaluations tend to be completed with a ranking at least of average or higher. HRP's should be vigilant to ensure that real evaluations are being done and that meaningful distinctions are drawn between different levels of performance and behaviour.

7. Employees who are having trouble should be put on a monitoring program with periodic interim evaluations completed according to a pre-set schedule – typically on a quarterly basis.

8. In every case, a supervisor should be required to meet with an employee who s/he has evaluated in order to explain the evaluation and listen to the employee's feedback. An employee should have an opportunity to add his or her own comments to the evaluation form.

Merit Pay

It is very difficult in a unionized operation to pay on any basis other than in accordance with a classification structure, with some recognition given to improvements in performance that are normal over the first few years of service in each classification. In such cases, where the first few years of service bring increases within a classification, they are usually automatic and do not depend on the actual performance of an employee.

If you could get agreement from the union on reasonable criteria to use in order to determine merit increases, you could implement a merit pay system. Naturally, the starting point is to have a proper wage grid. This is what a wage grid might look like in a manufacturing operation, with five classifications and six pay levels per classification, the last two being merit levels:

Classification	Prob'y	Start	1 year	2 years	Merit 1	Merit 2
Labourer	$10.50	$11.00	$11.50	$12.00	$12.50	$13.00+
Operator	$12.50	$13.00	$13.50	$14.00	$14.50	$15.00+
Ship/Receive	$13.50	$14.00	$14.50	$15.00	$15.50	$16.00+
Set Up	$14.50	$15.00	$15.50	$16.00	$16.50	$17.00+
Skilled	$18.50	$19.00	$19.50	$20.00	$20.50	$21.00+

The above grid could be easily translated into an office or service situation. Note that, even if you cannot negotiate merit increases, the grid is still useful as a model of using wage steps that increase wages both for higher classifications and also, to some extent, for greater service with the employer, and possibly even within each classification.

There are a few common features, which I recommend, but which are obviously not fixed in stone and entirely subject to the particular characteristics of each workplace and the normal give and take during collective bargaining:

- There is an initial pay raise after completion of the probationary period.
- The standard top rate is the 2-year rate (in the above grid — you may be able to build in more or less service before the top rate is achieved). If employees move to the next higher classification, then they would go to the probationary rate for that classification unless they were in receipt of merit pay, in which case they would go to the start rate or the next higher rate, depending on the amount of merit pay that had been received. Naturally, the merit pay would be lost with the promotion. Even in a grid without merit pay, the employer's goal should be to move a promoted employee to the bottom of the next higher classification, so long as the employee gets the same or (better) the next higher wage rate.
- The rates are fixed, and should be followed for the most part, to avoid perceived favouritism, although the second merit rate

allows for discretion (which could mean a number of additional merit levels, although it could easily get out of hand). In some unionized workplaces (the clear minority), wage levels are treated as minimum levels and the employer has the unfettered right to establish higher pay rates. In most unionized workplaces, it would be a violation of the collective agreement to pay above the negotiated rates or to accelerate movement from left to right through the grid.

- It may not make sense to start a qualified worker at the probationary rate, especially for higher rated classifications where the probationary rate may not be high enough to get a skilled applicant to accept employment. Sensible or not, in most workplaces you would need the union's agreement to start a qualified worker at an advanced step on the grid.

Here are three points that might not be obvious from looking at the grid example above:

- General increases normally will be negotiated to take place on an annual basis and would apply across the wage grid. The annual basis is convenient and normal, but not necessary. If it is agreed that a workplace needs a wage "catch-up", then semi-annual increases may be used to spread out the cost. If, on the other hand, wages are too high or the employer is in financial difficulty, then you may get agreement to wage freezes, sometimes with lump sum payments that do not raise wages in the grid.
- Careful consideration should be given to whether increases should be flat rate increases, which are easily understood by workers, but would shrink the relative difference between steps on the grid and between classifications. The alternative, which maintains the differences, is to have percentage increases across the board. It is possible to give different increases to different classifications, although that is not always easy for a union to sell to its members.
- When a wage grid is first established (usually in a first collective agreement), there often can be significant problems fitting current pay rates into a model grid. This can be solved with patience and creativity. I have often used red circles, yellow circles and green circles to help get everyone sorted out. Red circles freeze an employee at his or her current rate

until the classification catches up. Green circles freeze the differential between the current rate and the classification rate. Yellow circles are in between and shrink the differential over time, typically a period of two or three years.

Corrective Action Plan ("CAP")

The implementation and administration of a corrective action plan ("CAP") or system of discipline can be a difficult and unpleasant responsibility. Certainly, it can be the most obvious aspect of the management team's relationship with workers and their union.

The purpose of a CAP is to provide management with a system to help maintain the workplace rules and the standards of behaviour and performance that are considered to be necessary to ensure the orderly and efficient conduct of the employer's business. The rules and standards must be job-related or have a solid operational and business basis. They must be fully communicated to the workforce or generally understood as normal community standards. The workforce must also know that failure to conform to the standards or to obey the rules in the workplace will lead to corrective action at a level that will be determined by the employer to be appropriate on consideration of all relevant facts and circumstances.

At the risk of being obvious, the CAP only works if there is something that can be corrected. If an employee is doing his or her best, but simply lacks the qualifications, skill, ability (including physical ability) or intelligence to perform the job at the required standard, then the best CAP in the world is not going to be much help. There are other actions that can and should be taken, but they are not in the nature of a disciplinary system. We will consider this further in section 7(d) below.

If there is something to correct, it is important that the employer should be committed to take appropriate action. If a supervisor is not prepared to enforce adherence to a rule or standard, s/he is condoning its contravention, and so too is the entire management team.

Discipline is supposed to be corrective in nature, which is why I suggest calling the disciplinary system a CAP. Discipline should not be punitive. Employers are not meant to be the moral conscience of their employees. A CAP is used with employees as one method that will help achieve the performance that management considers to be necessary in order to achieve operational objectives. In essence, the purpose of the CAP is to help create more efficient and more effective employees, for the benefit of the organization and for the benefit of the employees themselves. Most importantly, the primary purpose of the CAP is to encourage employees to perform at the standards established by management. A CAP should not be used simply to create a paper trail to support a dismissal for just cause, although dismissal may be the result if the employee does not improve performance in response to the corrective actions that are taken.

CAP Fundamentals

The CAP is based on a fundamental principle of minimum force, which means that the employer should take the least serious corrective action thought necessary in order to achieve the objective of appropriate behaviour or improved performance. In this way, corrective action is also progressive. When an employee persists in inappropriate behaviour or poor performance following corrective action, then the original action was not sufficiently strong. As a result, progressively more severe corrective sanctions are imposed in order to reinforce management's concern, as well as to provide the employee with ample opportunity to improve before the final act of dismissal.

Here is what a typical CAP might look like for an employee who continues to violate the safety policy and the procedures established under that policy:

Step 1: oral warning with memorandum to file (although an oral warning is a step up from oral counselling, this still may be insufficient for a safety violation)

Step 2: written warning

Step 3: one-day suspension without pay

Step 4: three-day suspension without pay

Step 5: five-day suspension without pay and final warning

Step 6: dismissal for just cause, without notice, pay in lieu of notice or any other termination pay.[dismissal is also referred to as discharge or termination from employment]

There are a few points that bear noting from the above:

- depending on the seriousness of the infraction, you would not have to start at Step 1 and you could skip a step; indeed, the most serious infractions could lead directly to a dismissal;
- I recommend that suspensions be without pay; it is preferable if you make this clear in the CAP policy itself, which should be brought to the attention of new employees and the union, although it would be expected by the union;
- there are alternative CAP's that do not use unpaid suspensions; I generally discourage these; after over 50 years of arbitration experience in Canada, progressive discipline systems that include unpaid suspensions are normal and well understood by all participants in the system.
- Step 5 could be omitted or it could be an optional step, in which case the final warning would be Step 4.

Many workplaces would find it helpful to create a CAP form, such as the example on the following page:

[Employer logo]

CORRECTIVE ACTION PLAN

Name of employee: _____ *Date:* _____

Description of incident: _____

_____

_____

Applicable standard(s) or rule(s): _____

_____

_____

Date and level of prior corrective action: _____

_____

_____

Corrective action in this case: _____

Date/shift of return to work (if applicable): _____

This corrective action will remain on your record for two years and will be removed after that time, provided that no other corrective action is required in the meantime OR This corrective action will remain on your record indefinitely.

Please be advised that further situations that require corrective action could lead to more severe levels of corrective action up to and including dismissal for cause.

Please contact your supervisor or union steward if you have any questions.

Signature of Supervisor/Manager: _____ *Date:* _____

Name and Position of Supervisor/Manager: _____

I have received and read this corrective action: _____

_____ *Employee's Signature*

_____

_____*Union Steward*

CAP Levels

The six steps from the above example can be collapsed into four basic CAP levels:

1. *Oral counselling, followed by an oral reprimand or warning:*

    - Oral counselling is normally used for a first offence or where the facts and circumstances indicate that more severe CAP levels are not warranted, such as when a normally punctual employee arrives late for work.
    - Oral counselling is sometimes thought of as a kinder, gentler form of oral warning. It is typically one on one and often very brief. In the best meetings, the worker would be invited to recommend a solution for the problem.
    - A cautionary note: supervisors should never have one-on-one meetings with employees behind closed doors, unless the office is a windowed office, and especially if the employee is of the other gender. In an oral warning session, it is good form in any event to have a second member of the management team in attendance. Depending on the requirements of the collective agreement, a union steward may also have to be present, although it is typical that the union steward is not required until, at least, a more formal verbal warning.
    - Although no official notice of the incident is placed on the employee's file, the supervisor should retain some form of record for future reference in the event the employee does not correct the sub-standard behaviour — a simple note should do, recording the employee's name, the date of the discussion and a brief summary of what took place.
    - If the supervisor uses some kind of form or a memorandum to file, especially following a more formal meeting to deliver an oral warning, then a copy should be provided to the employee (this is sometimes referred to as a "written verbal").

2. *Written Reprimand or Warning:*

    - A written warning normally is issued when the oral counselling or warning has not elicited the improvement required of the employee and another infraction of the rule has occurred. Therefore, reinforcement of the warning is required. It also may be issued for a first offence that warrants a sanction more severe than an oral reprimand, such as breaching a relatively minor safety rule or a heated verbal altercation with a co-worker.

A written warning should document at least the following five points:

- briefly describe the misconduct (follow the standard tools of reporting — who, what, why, when and where);
- identify the standard or rule that was breached;
- list any prior warnings;
- indicate the corrective action selected (i.e. written warning); and
- warn of the consequences of continuing or repeating the behaviour: that further corrective action would follow, up to and including dismissal.

One copy of the warning goes to the employee; a second copy is retained on file.

---

3. *Suspension without Pay:*

- A suspension without pay normally is imposed when an employee persists in unsatisfactory conduct or behaviour, even after repeated efforts by management to have the employee correct the sub-standard performance. A suspension also may be imposed for a first occurrence of a serious act of misconduct, such as fighting on the job, insubordinate behaviour, and more serious safety infractions. Written confirmation of the suspension should be provided to the employee in much the same form as a written warning; a second copy is retained on file.
- I suggest using odd-numbered suspensions of one day, three days or five days. That way, if there is a grievance about the severity of the suspension and additional mitigating facts are identified, then you may be able to settle the grievance by rolling back the corrective action without having to return to the prior level of corrective action taken. A progressive CAP could repeat a level, but it should never go backward and it

generally should go forward, especially once you are at the level of suspension.

- I see little point in a suspension that is longer than five days. Unless there are special circumstances, or you are agreeing to reinstate an employee, subject to time served, five days (perhaps even three days) should be plenty as the most serious corrective action short of dismissal, especially when combined with a clear final warning.

4. *Dismissal:*

The following discussion about dismissal is entirely within the context of the CAP and is not meant to refer to economic dismissals or dismissals due to the workers' inability to continue in employment (a "frustration" of employment, which is considered further in section 7(d)(iii) below). As such, this discussion contemplates two kinds of situations:

- The first kind of CAP situation arises from progressive discipline, in which a final incident, combined with a record of prior discipline, is justification for dismissal of an unsatisfactory employee.
- The second kind of CAP situation is a single incident discharge arising from a particularly serious act of misconduct.

Here are the key points that deal with dismissal under the CAP:

- The dismissal of the employee normally will take place after all efforts at correcting poor behaviour or sub-standard performance have failed. In some cases, the act of misconduct is of such a serious nature that management feels that it is left with no other option. In those cases, a dismissal for cause may issue, even though it is a first offence. Some examples include a serious breach of trust, such as theft or fraud, or where an employee physically assaults a manager or attacks another employee with a tool or weapon.
- In a unionized workplace, it is unlikely that there would be a grievance until a written warning is issued. Even then, all that the employer has to prove is that misconduct took place that merited some disciplinary response. That is a pretty low standard, so long as you have your facts

straight. As a result, a unionized employer is almost unfettered in its use of a CAP at least to the point of the first suspension. Even then, if corrective action has been progressive, a one-day suspension is the next obvious step, again, so long as you can prove misconduct.

- With freedom comes responsibility. To avoid alienating the workforce and getting mired in grievances even for low-level discipline, a CAP has to be administered in a consistent and reasonable manner. Individual decisions to correct behaviour or performance must not be arbitrary, discriminatory, or motivated by bad faith. Given the importance of perception in applying such a system, an employer must strive to appear fair and balanced in its approach.

- As would be usual for any step of the CAP, when imposing dismissal, the decision-maker and another member of the management team should meet with the employee and a union steward to inform him or her of the action taken and the reasons for it. Written confirmation also should be delivered to the employee, using the format first described above for a written warning; a copy of the letter should be placed on the file.

- As an alternative to dismissal, or as a possible settlement, you may consider continuing employment or reinstating an employee subject to conditions, which may also include a monitoring period. A conditional reinstatement or continuation of employment normally would include an agreement that a future dismissal could not be grieved if, in fact, the employee breaches the fundamental conditions of ongoing employment.

When Corrective Action is Appropriate

As noted above, there is no point in taking corrective action at all unless there is something to correct. As subsequently discussed, if there is a decision to take corrective action, then there are four basic levels that could apply and at least a couple of different steps at each of the first level of oral counselling or warning and the third level of unpaid suspensions. The employer's response to a first offence may vary according to the seriousness of the misconduct. Similarly, where an employee has previously received corrective action, the facts and circumstances of a current incident may indicate that more serious corrective action is warranted than simply proceeding to the next step.

Unless penalties for breaches of established rules and standards are specified by the collective agreement (which is rare) or the employer's policies, procedures or rules, decisions regarding the appropriate level of corrective action always will involve a degree of subjectivity. In the pursuit of consistency, you will want to minimize this inevitable subjectivity through a suitable investigation of the facts and circumstances of each case. Keep in mind that we are not talking about anything like a criminal investigation, except in those situations where there has been something like theft or assault, in which case the police may become involved in any event. Those exceptions aside we are usually talking about simple workplace misconduct – a failure to meet standards. For the most part, the processes of investigation and decision-making should be straightforward and prompt – usually within a matter of hours or days.

As well as the collective agreement or any policies, procedures or rules you may have regarding appropriate levels of discipline, there is one particular situation where the level of corrective action may be pre-determined. If an employee is subject to a serious suspension or is given another chance through reinstatement to the workplace following a dismissal, that should be accompanied by a formal settlement that includes terms and conditions for continued employment or for reinstatement. This is often the case with non-disciplinary absenteeism situations (further considered in section 7(d)(iii) below), as well as in situations that involve substance abuse. Each set of terms and conditions will be based on individual facts, but plans for ongoing employment should have at least these features:

- A threshold requirement to go through rehabilitation in substance abuse cases.
- A requirement for ongoing medical treatment and reporting and, in substance abuse cases, post-rehabilitation care (such as group meetings, like AA).
- A requirement to avoid the originating problem (such as drinking or failing to take prescribed medication to control a permanent condition).
- A requirement to follow applicable attendance procedures.

- A minimum time period, typically two years and subject to extension.

Failure to follow the above features could result in dismissal for cause without further notice and without the right to grieve the consequence. In this way, an alcoholic who goes through a rehabilitation program would be subject to termination, not for the alcoholism (which is a disability covered by human rights provisions), but for choosing to violate the terms and conditions of ongoing employment, which is misconduct. The only basis for a grievance in such an example or generally would be if there were a factual dispute about whether or not the terms and conditions actually were violated.

Although very effective, these "last chance" agreements may run afoul of human rights legislation if not carefully drafted. This is one of the situations where the assistance of a labour lawyer could be very worthwhile.

There are three basic steps in making a decision about corrective action. All three steps are derived from the expectation that management will be responsible for establishing the facts of the case and, if there is a legal proceeding, then management will have the onus of proof, either as a matter of law or as a matter of evidence, depending on the proceeding. Here are the steps:

- Has the employer been able to establish what happened, as a matter of fact? If so, is the employer in a position to identify the employee who may be at fault?
- Is any corrective action warranted? Did the employee engage in misconduct? Could the employee have done something different or better had s/he wanted to or had a better choice been made, when such choice was readily available to the employee?
- If some corrective action is warranted, what is most appropriate, in consideration of the principles of minimum force and progressive action?

Conducting an Investigation

If it seems appropriate, you should investigate cases of misconduct or sub-standard performance promptly and completely. You should try to stay objective. Keep an open mind. Make your decisions at the end of the investigation. Try to avoid investigating simply to support decisions you made right at the outset.

Each employee is responsible for his or her own actions and behaviour. Employees must not be randomly disciplined. You cannot punish the entire workforce simply because you are unable to identify the culprit. Responsibility is determined by the facts identified in the investigation. In gathering facts required for the decision steps set out above, always follow the W5 rule, as per this diagram:

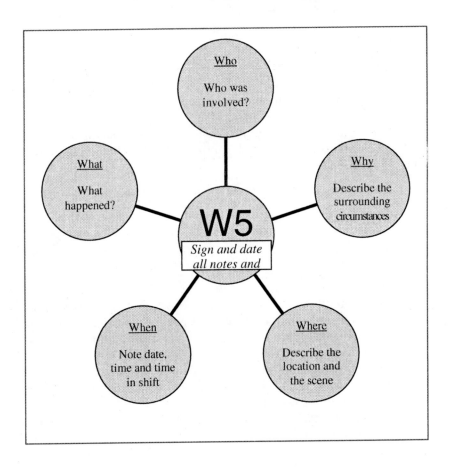

Here are key sources for your facts:

1. Statements of witnesses with direct knowledge of the incident or misconduct, whether as participants or spectators.
2. Statements of persons who were not witnesses, but who have reliable second-hand information. This would be called "hearsay" in a legal proceeding, but is quite useful in a workplace investigation, provided that you remember to treat it as "second-best" information.
3. Documentation pertaining to the misconduct, whether pre-existing or created in the normal course of business at the time of, or shortly following, the incident.
4. Other kinds of evidence, including photographs, videotape, diagrams, and objects.
5. Indirect or circumstantial evidence that should stand up to the following tests:

   • it should point to the employee as having committed the offence or misconduct; and
   • it should exclude any other reasonable explanation, such as a determination that another employee could have committed the offence as easily.

Here are three key points about the investigation process:

1. At the end of every investigation, the employee who has been identified as the target for corrective action should be interviewed, even if s/he has been interviewed earlier in the process. Three aspects of this interview are important to understand:

   • the point of the interview is to provide the employee with an opportunity to tell his or her side of the story; this is not a cross-examination, but a final chance for the employee to give an explanation for what appears to be poor behaviour or unsatisfactory performance; and
   • the investigation interview should be separated from the subsequent disciplinary interview, when the employee is advised of the corrective action – there should be at least a ten minute break, time to get a coffee or some other kind of pause; sometimes the break will be longer, but it should not be any longer than a couple of days.

- A union steward is not generally entitled to participate in an investigation interview; however, it is often a good idea to include a union steward in the interview, especially for serious or contentious situations. A union steward is almost certainly required to attend the disciplinary meeting. Depending on the language in the collective agreement, discipline could be null and void if the union steward is not at the disciplinary meeting. This would be a tough pill for the employer to swallow at arbitration several months later, especially in a discharge case due to a serious infraction. Not only would the "bad egg" return to work, but also s/he would return with full back-pay.

2. In some cases, it is appropriate to suspend an employee pending investigation. If you determine that an employee should not be present in the workplace because of a serious incident, but you have not had time to complete a suitable investigation, you may tell an employee not to attend work in the meantime. Depending on the circumstances, this suspension could be with or without pay; I generally recommend that it be without pay. In most cases, it should be for a period of only a few days. Some cases have featured much longer suspensions pending investigation, especially if there is a serious incident that involves public trust.

3. In most cases, you should aim to complete your investigation and determine the extent of corrective action, if any, within a week of the incident or circumstances giving rise to the investigation.

Mitigating Circumstances: Fitting Corrective Action to the Misconduct

The severity of the misconduct, misbehaviour or poor performance of an employee will have a significant impact on the level of corrective action that is assessed. Breaching safety rules, assault or the intentional destruction of the employer's property are considered to be more serious acts of misconduct than lateness, and, for that reason alone, would tend to result in more severe corrective action. Several other mitigating or extenuating factors should be considered before settling on appropriate corrective action, such as:

- seniority or length of service;

105

- problems away from the workplace;
- the potential for rehabilitation, which may be largely established by the employee's reaction to the investigation process and his or her willingness to accept responsibility;
- provocation by other employees, including supervisors, or other circumstances that contributed to the situation;
- an apparent need for additional training;
- concerns about flaws in the investigation process itself; and
- most important, the prior record of corrective action that has been taken in respect of this employee; on this final factor, there are at least four points to keep in mind:

   (i)   although you may decide to separate out certain performance issues and deal with them on their own – attendance management being the most obvious – there is no need in general to have different streams of corrective action to deal with different categories of misconduct; you should have one main stream of corrective action in which past misconduct of any category is relevant to the present determination;

   (ii)   as a counter-balance to the point above, the more recent and the more similar the prior corrective action, the more significant should be its impact on the current situation;

   (iii)   at some point, prior corrective action should become stale, unless it deals with the most serious of offences; a "sunset" clause is normal in a collective agreement; generally speaking, two years is a suitable time frame, so that if an employee does not engage in misconduct during that period, then prior corrective action should be removed from the record or at least declared to be stale; a union often will try to bargain a shorter period so that the sun will set after 18 months or a year of no discipline;

   (iv)   one of the important aspects of corrective action that is progressive is that even relatively minor misconduct could lead to a dismissal if there is a significant record of prior and reasonably current corrective action; in common parlance, this is know as the straw that broke the camel's back or the brick that bent the axle; in labour relations, this is referred to as dismissal based on a culminating incident.

Once you have taken corrective action, you should not take other or more severe corrective action for the same incident of misconduct. You should be sure to explain this clearly to your front-line supervisors. If, for example, a supervisor is faced with a disruptive or inebriated employee on an afternoon or night shift, the proper action is to send the employee home without pay pending investigation. Many supervisors have made the mistake of telling the employee that s/he is suspended for the balance of the shift, which fixes the corrective action. If it is subsequently determined that the employee has a record of corrective action and should have been dismissed, the argument of cause for dismissal may have been compromised by the supervisor's initial announcement. This trap for unwary employers sometimes takes on the name of the equivalent concept in criminal law: "double jeopardy".

Sometimes new or additional facts are obtained after the imposition of the discipline, which may lead to having the penalty reassessed. In such cases, if you hope to succeed at arbitration with an argument of just cause for dismissal and avoid a claim of double jeopardy, then you should be able to show that the new or additional facts could not have been determined in the course of a reasonable investigation prior to the original corrective action.

Summary of an Effective CAP

- Ensure that your employees and any unions in your workplace are informed of the rules and standards to which they must conform. The rules and standards are likely entirely within management's rights and not affected by collective agreement provisions, so you should be able to have consistent rules and standards for all of your employees in the workplace, unionized or not.

- Enforce these rules and standards in a consistent and equitable fashion.

- React in a timely manner to all breaches of the rules and standards.

- Thoroughly investigate incidents of misconduct and ensure that the employee who is alleged to have engaged in the misconduct receives a full and fair opportunity to provide you with an explanation.

- Act promptly, especially in serious cases and/or if you have suspended an employee pending investigation.

- Base your decision as to the appropriate corrective action on all the facts and circumstances of the current situation. Remember to give careful consideration to possible mitigating or extenuating circumstances and to the record.

- Discuss with the employee the action that you are taking in the privacy of your office, preferably with another management witness in attendance, and almost certainly with a union steward present as a matter of right.

- Create a written record, except for cases of preliminary oral counselling, where it may suffice for you to write a note to yourself.

- Follow up on corrective action. Take further action if it is warranted or let an employee know that his/her performance is improving.

- Make sure that supervisors and managers consult with the HRP to review the proposed corrective action and to comment on the letter or form; also ensure that the decision-maker has the required authority to take action.

The Final Break from Employment: a Review of Dismissal Scenarios

It is increasingly rare that people retire from the company or organization where they first had full-time employment. For employees at all levels, and especially at higher levels, it is normal to change jobs; perhaps many times over the 40 or 50 years that is a typical adult work span. There are many reasons why an employee would leave employment, and these were summarized in section 3(a)(i) above, which dealt with the common law of contracts as it applies to employment. This review will focus on the three key types of employer-initiated dismissals in which work performance is the central issue.

Disciplinary Discharge or Dismissal for Just Cause

Whether or not you use the CAP, or something similar to it, you may have a situation in which an employee's misconduct (either a single incident or a series of incidents of sub-standard behaviour) is so significant that it shatters any prospect for a viable employment relationship. Trust is gone. Workplace relationships are poisoned. The very presence of the employee in the workplace is worse than neutral, it is detrimental to the performance of other employees, and of the overall group.

Sometimes old words perfectly capture the sense of a situation. Here, the word is *moribund*. By the action or actions of the employee, the employee relationship is essentially dead. The problem is proving cause, especially if you have not used a CAP, or if the facts of the single or final incident are in dispute, or if the significance of the misconduct is challenged.

Dismissal for Non-Performance: Non-Disciplinary Absenteeism

The issue of absenteeism and its consequences for an employment relationship was introduced in section 4(c) above. This section will provide further details about how to proceed with a dismissal in those kinds of situations. If done correctly, such dismissals stand a reasonable chance of succeeding without giving rise to a legitimate claim for damages. As with many employment situations, but especially because these are dismissals that have human rights and possibly other statutory implications, you should probably get legal advice from the outset, or at least before taking the final action.

If an employee is ill or injured and absent from the workplace for an indefinite period, there comes a time when the employer can fairly conclude that there is no reasonable expectation that the employee will be able to resume employment, even if the work is modified to accommodate medical restrictions. It is typical to wait two years before making such a determination. The period of time may vary according to disability plans and workers' compensation situations if you are dealing with a compensable situation.

For most cases, there is a two-step dismissal process:

1. Make sure that you get current medical information. Let the employee know, by letter, what medical information you have on file, and that the information indicates that the employee is unable to return to work. Invite the employee to provide further or different medical information. Make clear to the employee that, unless there is information that indicates the realistic possibility of a return in the foreseeable future, then employment will be terminated. Clarify the status of any disability coverage. Provide the employee with a timeframe for response, typically two weeks and indicate that, if there is no response, you will assume that your information is correct.

2. Act promptly on whatever response you get, including a failure to respond within the timeframe. If the information suggests that employment may resume in the near future, then you should become very active on the file, to ensure that you are not simply being placed into an indefinite holding pattern. Insist on dates for further medical reports, within weeks, not months, and consider getting an independent medical review or even an independent medical examination if you have concerns about the quality of the medical reporting.

The other kind of non-performance due to absenteeism is when an employee is frequently absent for short periods. Dealing with this kind of absenteeism becomes complicated if some of the absences are due to workplace injuries or illnesses. As well, Ontario's emergency leave provisions, introduced in September 2001, effectively provide employees with a free ride for up to ten days per year. That said, for most cases, there is a three-step dismissal process, with each step featuring a meeting and a follow-up letter:

1. Introduce the problem, with statistics going back a year or two. You will need good attendance records, and you should relate the employee to his or her own group (such as a production unit or an office unit). Indicate that the employee's attendance is below the norm. Clarify that this is not disciplinary — you are not challenging the reasons for absence. Recommend that the employee get medical assistance to deal with any underlying problems. Provide the employee with a timeframe for improvement, typically two or three months. Warn that failure to improve attendance could lead to dismissal. Follow up with the employee at the end of that period or in the meantime, if the problem continues to be serious.
2. Follow up. If the problem is the same or worse, then you should provide a final monitoring period of the same length (two or three months). Make it as clear as possible that a failure to improve attendance will likely result in dismissal.
3. Dismiss or follow up for the final time at the end of the second monitoring period. In some cases, you might give one last chance to an employee. A proper exercise of managerial discretion requires that each case be considered on its own merits. If an employee appears to be making a real effort to improve attendance, then you should be patient. As with progressive discipline, when you are dealing with a situation of frequent short-term absenteeism, the goal is to improve the employee's attendance, not to terminate employment.

Dismissal for Poor Performance, but Not for Just Cause

It is sometimes the case that an employee is willing to work hard and to do well, but simply is not able to perform the work at a reasonable standard. These cases are fairly rare and can be difficult to prove; however, in every case of poor performance, an employer always should examine carefully whether it is misconduct or a lack of ability that is producing the poor results.

If it seems to be a lack of ability, an employer should take the situation outside of the CAP. Instead, the employer should treat the situation in much the same way as it does frequent short-term absenteeism:

1. Introduce the problem. You should meet with the employee, usually along with a union steward, to describe the nature of the poor performance. Ideally, you will have an objective basis, at least to some degree, for your concerns; however, a subjective assessment is completely acceptable, although more difficult to establish, so long as it is reasonable and not arbitrary, discriminatory or formed in bad faith. Usually with the full participation of the employee and the steward, you will then come up with an action plan, which may include training, a "buddy system", close monitoring and frequent reporting. The meeting will be summarized in writing shortly afterwards.

2. Follow up. At the end of a suitable monitoring period, typically six to eight weeks, you would have a second meeting to discuss progress. If the situation is the same or worse, then you should caution the employee that s/he will not remain in the position absent significant improvement. If the situation is better, then you will try to establish patterns and procedures that will lock in the improvement for the long term.

3. Demote, dismiss or arrange for follow-up for the final time following the second monitoring period. If the situation is the same or worse, you should bring it to an end, unless there is some reason to expect a turnaround. Although not likely covered by the collective agreement, convention would treat this situation as a lay-off, in which case the employee could use whatever bumping rights existed in accordance with the seniority provisions. Absent bumping rights, or at the insistence of the union, you may be faced with a non-disciplinary dismissal, or the employee could be placed on the recall list.

If there is still some reason to hope for a turnaround, you may want to provide for one last chance, although you should be looking at some very specific criteria for measuring success and, quite likely, a shorter monitoring period.

A Few Words About Settlements

Just cause for dismissal is hard to establish and will be challenged by the union in almost every case. Effective use of the CAP will provide significant assistance to an employer that is trying to move to the point of discharge, but most arbitrators are reluctant to find that there is no basis to re-establish a viable employment relationship. The stakes are high. Often an arbitrator will compromise and return a discharged employee to work without back-pay. Even then, it is something of a triumph for the union and the discharged employee on the day that s/he returns to the workplace. To say the least, this sends a mixed message to the other workers and is demoralizing to management. Worse yet, there is always the possibility that the arbitrator will order partial or full back-pay.

There are pressures on the worker and the union as well. Often, the reinstatement of a discharged worker would not be particularly welcome by the other workers. There is always the possibility that the worker will not be reinstated. Even if reinstated, the worker likely will be returning with a very heavy suspension and may be facing imminent dismissal for any degree of future misconduct. In a non-disciplinary situation, due to absenteeism or inability, reinstatement could have a significant and negative impact on the overall quality of your workforce.

Given the pressures on both sides, it is sometimes possible to negotiate a buy-out. It is galling for an employer to pay money to an employee who has been the author of his or her own misfortune; however, that is sometimes a prudent course of action. Such a settlement would be drafted to set no precedent as a matter of law. As a matter of workplace reality, each settlement sends a powerful message to the remaining employees — workers and supervisors alike. Employers have to be very careful about the messages that they create and must also work hard afterwards to manage the message.

The more usual settlement is to agree to reinstate the employee, without compensation, but usually without loss of seniority. Although the employer may experience the problems with reinstatement noted above, there are at least three advantages:
1. you get a certain result;
2. you can often negotiate much better conditions for reinstatement than would be ordered by an arbitrator; and

3. if poor performance or poor attendance continues, dismissal the next time around should be relatively straightforward.

Even in cases of reinstatement, which may not be an entirely satisfactory result, you are much better off than you would be had you failed to take action.

♦

CHAPTER 7

ENCOURAGING SUGGESTIONS AND
COMPLAINTS: GRIEVANCES AND ARBITRATIONS

There are no perfect workplaces. Every workplace is dynamic. Every workplace is full of challenges. Even the most positive workplaces will not have everyone headed in the same direction all the time. When there is conflict in the workplace between management and workers, there must be an avenue available to workers to bring forward complaints or concerns. Workers expect to be heard. If they have a valid basis for complaint, workers expect an effective and prompt remedy. If they are unsuccessful at first, workers expect at least a second level reconsideration of their complaint.

With an effective complaints procedure, management will find out about problems that were unknown or under-appreciated. In most cases, management will have the opportunity to intervene with solutions that are not costly and actually may benefit the organization. Mistakes can be corrected before any real damage is done. Opportunities can be realized before it is too late to gain the full benefit of a good idea.

In a unionized workplace, the complaints procedure is required by legislation and is a standard feature of every collective agreement. Management that is frustrated by the grievance and arbitration process should remember that it is much better than the alternative of unresolved labour disputes and wildcat work stoppages.

Complaints are Normal

One of the key responsibilities of management is to detect and, where possible, prevent problems or disputes from escalating into full-blown disputes. As is so often the case in matters of human resources management, the spotlight is on the front-line supervisor, who deals with the employees on a day-to-day basis. This is an especially important responsibility for supervisors in a unionized workplace, because unattended discontent creates fertile ground for potentially costly and disruptive grievances.

Even the best supervisors cannot avoid disputes or prevent complaints. Indeed, it is often very good supervisors who cause complaints because of their insistence on high standards of behaviour or performance. Anybody with teenage children would recognize that setting expectations and insisting on compliance is not always a path strewn with flowers. Some of your workers may not be much different from teenagers. In fact some of them still are teenagers or not much older than that and they are still learning to behave in an adult situation, such as a modern workplace.

There is nothing wrong with complaints. Think of them as just another way for employees to make suggestions about how the workplace should be managed. Not only will complaints alert the management team to potential problems, they are also a good way for employees to let off steam. While you do not want to encourage negativism and conflict in your workplace, you certainly should make it easy for employees to complain and to have their complaints resolved. Indeed, if you think of complaints as suggestions, then you may gain a new perspective on the grievance procedure as an evolution of the suggestion box.

Open the Door: Encourage Complaints and Limit Grievances

In a unionized workplace, the formal grievance procedure has a few different steps. The first step is the complaint, which then evolves into a written grievance. At the final step, it is open to either party (typically the union) to submit any unresolved dispute to binding arbitration by a neutral adjudicator. The objective for management in a unionized workplace is to encourage complaints while limiting grievances and arbitrations by encouraging the resolution of complaints at a very early stage.

In my view, it is insufficient to achieve this objective of encouraging complaints while limiting grievances simply by saying that you have an "open-door" policy. Often, your view that you have an open door may be nothing more than a vague hope that you are approachable. Your employees may have a much different perception. They may be shy and without self-confidence. They may have difficulty articulating their views and concerns. They may be afraid that complaints will diminish their standing in the workplace and affect their job security and opportunity for advancement. If you really do have an open-door policy that employees feel comfortable walking through, then you should have no difficulty making sure that open door is completely transparent and accessible to all.

Even the best open-door manager will not be able to measure up to the full advantages of a union grievance procedure. That is because open-door managers can only offer one-stop shopping. The best that an open-door manager can do will be to resolve the worker's issue or convince the worker that s/he has no real issue. By contrast, every grievance procedure features at least a second step and often a third or fourth step. These additional steps allow the employee to have an initial decision reconsidered at progressively higher levels of managerial authority.

This is what a typical grievance procedure looks like.

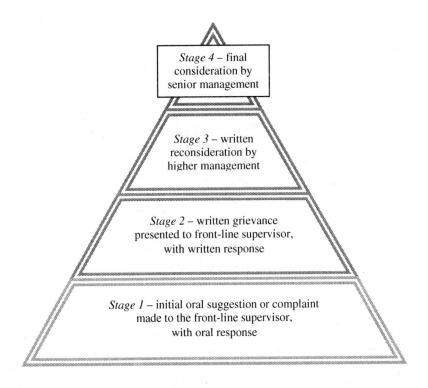

Stage 4 – final consideration by senior management

Stage 3 – written reconsideration by higher management

Stage 2 – written grievance presented to front-line supervisor, with written response

Stage 1 – initial oral suggestion or complaint made to the front-line supervisor, with oral response

It is important to note that the written grievance does not emerge until the second stage. You should always make room for an informal oral complaint at the initial stage.

Details of the Grievance Procedure

What distinguishes a unionized complaint procedure from any comparable procedure in non-union workplaces is the availability of arbitration at the end of the line. An arbitration hearing is a reasonably formal legal proceeding, in which the parties are the employer and the union, acting on its own behalf or on behalf of an employee. The arbitrator is typically a lawyer or a professional with experience and training in mediation and arbitration. The arbitrator is unbiased and neutral, and has no relationship with either party. In most cases, the arbitrator issues a written decision, often with detailed reasons. To a very limited extent, an arbitrator's decision could be reviewed in court, but generally, as a matter of fact and law, arbitral decisions are final and binding on the parties, and set a precedent for similar disputes between the two parties in question.

Most employers in non-union workplaces have nothing like arbitration to offer to their workers. Most employers in unionized workplaces try to avoid arbitration, sometimes at almost any cost. My own view is that management should be fearless about the prospect of arbitration. It is part of the cost of doing business. It is a cost for the union as well. In most cases, you will find that the union does not have much more appetite than the employer to race off to arbitration.

Let us look a little more closely at each of three points that are key features of the grievance procedure: time frames (which are usually set out in the collective agreement), the grievance form, and grievance meetings. The following section, 8(d), will review the arbitration itself:

1. *Time Frames*: Complaints should be made when they actually arise or soon thereafter – a matter of days at most. In the same way, the initial response should be right away or within a couple of days. It should be stressed that it is absolutely essential that there be some response. There is no excuse for a failure to respond. If a supervisor needs more information, then the employee should be advised of that and a response should be forthcoming as soon as the information is obtained. Each of the subsequent steps should take place within days, or at most a couple of weeks (especially at higher steps, where meetings may be scheduled). It is always the same process: the employee makes

or advances the complaint, management considers it at each level, and then management makes a response.

2. *Grievance Form*: Here is a sample form, typically supplied by the union; there is often room on the form to advance the complaint to second or third steps, but it is really only completion at the initial step that is important:

3. *Grievance Meetings*: At the very least, there are two practices that can go a long way to avoiding the need for arbitration. First, senior management should be involved in a meaningful way at the final step. This could be the HRP, if considered to be a senior position within the operation, or a senior operations manager, such as a plant manager in a manufacturing facility. Second, at the final step, and perhaps the final couple of steps, there should be a meeting where an employee and/or the union has an opportunity to present the issue. This may be a requirement of the collective agreement, in which case it is important to avoid having the meeting become merely a formal routine.

GRIEVANCE FORM

Name of employee: _____ *Date:* _____

Description of complaint: _____

_____

_____

Applicable collective agreement provisions: _____

_____

_____

Action or remedy requested: _____

_____

_____

Signature of Employee: _____*Steward:* _____

Response by the Employer, with reasons: _____

_____

Signature of Supervisor/Manager: _____ *Date:* _____

Name and Position of Supervisor/Manager: _____

I have received and read this response: _____

Employee's Signature

I am satisfied _____OR I wish to have my complaint considered at a higher level

Arbitration

If arbitration cannot be avoided, understand that it is a legal process, even though it takes place in a relatively informal setting. The arbitration procedure can be usefully summarized by this simple phrase: "PING-PONG-ping". Except as specifically described below, the party that has the onus is PING-ping. The other party is PONG. Onus is very straightforward: if it is a case of discipline or discharge, then the employer must go first and must establish at least the basic elements of just cause. In all other cases, the union has the onus to establish a violation of the collective agreement. Other than determining who starts (and who finishes), onus should not mean that much in most cases. The party that has the onus is usually able to present sufficient evidence to shift the real burden of proof to the other party. Once that is done, each side will call all of the evidence that is considered to be relevant to a determination of the issue(s).

Arbitration hearings have a preliminary stage, then three normal stages. At the preliminary stage, one party or other (usually the employer) can object to the jurisdiction of the arbitrator. A common basis for an objection is that the grievance was not advanced in accordance with the time limits and processes in the collective agreement. Another basis for an objection is that the grievance does not involve a matter that is properly the subject of arbitration, either because it does not involve a violation of the collective agreement or does not otherwise arise under an applicable statute. In this latter respect, an arbitrator would have jurisdiction to consider complaints of a union member arising under employment statutes such as employment standards, human rights or health and safety.

Regardless of where the onus lies in the main part of the case, for the purposes of the preliminary objection, PING-ping is the party that brings the objection. The objection may mirror the three stages of the main part of the hearing and a determination may be required before the arbitration can proceed to the main part of the case. This is known as bifurcation and, for practical purposes, usually means that the hearing will take at least two days, to be separated by a number of weeks at least. In some cases, the parties may agree that the objection should be determined at the end of the case. Although it may seem peculiar, it is the arbitrator who has to determine whether or not s/he has jurisdiction.

After the preliminary stage (if any), the three normal stages of an arbitration hearing are:

1. *Opening Statements:* Whoever has the onus is PING-ping. That party provides the first opening statement to the arbitrator. The purpose of the opening statement is to identify to the arbitrator the main aspects of your case that you intend to prove through evidence. As well, if there are agreed facts or documents that can go in on consent (at least the collective agreement and the grievance, and often much more), then this should be done in the opening. You should not argue the legal aspects of the case, although it is normal to refer to relevant articles in the collective agreement and to sketch out the main theory of the case.

   PONG follows PING. If anything is raised by PONG that was not anticipated by PING, then there is one final opportunity, which I call "ping". It is in small letters, because the point of this final opportunity is simply to respond to unforeseen points that were not dealt with at the outset. Ping is not intended to repeat what has already been said, and there is no excuse for ambushing PONG by withholding points that were readily foreseeable. Ambush is not much of a danger during this first stage, but becomes much more serious in the middle and final stages. Indeed, often there is no ping at all in the opening.

2. *Evidence:* PING (the party with the onus) has to proceed first with all of its witnesses. The examination of each witness is a miniature PING-PONG-ping, as there is examination-in-chief, followed by cross-examination, and completed with a limited right of re-examination. Witnesses will provide first-hand accounts and (less satisfactorily) second-hand or hearsay accounts of facts relevant to the situation in issue. Witnesses may also have to identify documents and things that will be relied on as evidence in addition to the oral testimony.

   Here is a summary of each of the miniature PING-PONG-ping parts that are in play during the presentation of the evidence of each witness:

   • Examination-in-chief features open-ended questions that are designed to prompt the witness, but should not suggest the answer in any specific way (except on non-contentious points) the answer that you want the witness to give. It may help to picture the role of the counsel or representative as a guide who is proceeding with a light ahead of the witness down a dark path. The guide shows the way, but it is up to the witness to travel the distance that is required.

- Cross-examination features leading questions that are specifically designed to suggest the answer that the opposing counsel or representative wants to obtain. In a good cross-examination, the answers should be very short — "yes", "no", "I don't know", "I don't remember". The primary purposes of cross-examination are to discredit the testimony by putting the credibility or reliability of the witness into question, to blunt the testimony (take out some of the sting) or to introduce new evidence. Here, you could picture the role of the counsel or representative as someone taking a nasty dog out for a walk using a choke collar and a short leash. The objective is to get the dog to go where you want the dog to go. The dog, being surly and powerful may not go there very willingly. Sometimes you have to trick the dog with guile and cleverness when brute strength is ineffective.

- As introduced above, re-examination can only deal with issues raised during cross-examination that were not dealt with in chief and could not have been reasonably foreseen. You can usually get away with a few questions, even if they cross the line; however, a re-examination of any length should be challenged by the other side as inappropriate and often will be disallowed.

Once PING has called all of its witnesses, it is up to PONG to call its witnesses, if any. In some cases, PONG will be satisfied with the evidence and will choose to call no witnesses. In most cases where the facts are not agreed, PONG will call at least one witness. Naturally, in that case, you get a miniature PONG-PING-pong, such that PONG-pong is in the role of conducting the examination-in-chief and the re-examination.

Once PONG has called its witnesses, ping has the right to call additional witnesses, who may be new or witnesses who have already testified. As should be familiar, this is a limited right that is intended to deal only with new evidentiary issues raised by the PONG witnesses that could not have been reasonably foreseen at the outset by PING. Repeating evidence or trying to use ping as the other part of a sandwich in an ambush attempt is objectionable and would be disallowed in most cases.

3. *Argument:* As you would expect, PING goes first and ping goes last (in a limited way) with PONG in the middle. This is the opportunity to pull out the most relevant facts from the evidence and to interpret the evidence in a manner that supports the argument that you are trying to make based in any, some or all of the collective agreement, relevant statutory provisions, or prevailing jurisprudence. Jurisprudence can include legal texts, arbitration decisions, or court decisions. Only court decisions that relate to the jurisdiction in which the hearing is proceeding and that are on point ought to be binding (although they are typically easy to distinguish). Otherwise, what legal writers or other arbitrators say can be compelling and may be persuasive, but it is certainly not binding.

Issues for Grievances

The most usual grievances deal with the following issues or situations:

- the improper interpretation, application or general administration of different aspects of the framework, especially the collective agreement or applicable statutory provisions;
- improper classification, in that the worker claims to be doing a different kind of work than that for which s/he is being paid;
- unjust discipline, especially cases of unpaid suspension or dismissal.

Even if you have a comprehensive framework and a collective agreement that is both reasonable and well communicated, all of this is written and communicated in English. The English language is incapable of capturing all of the factual permutations and combinations that can arise with human interactions in a workplace. Indeed, management does not want a framework that is so clear and so detailed that there is no room for the exercise of discretion. For its part, the union will often accept a provision in the collective agreement that leaves room for interpretation and plenty of room for the exercise of managerial discretion — sometimes because this is the best that it can achieve, but often because it would be tiresome and even self-defeating to try to cover all possible scenarios. Both parties live in a perpetual tug of war, where the framework that lies within the rights of management is constantly being challenged by a collective agreement that seeks to restrict the exercise of those rights.

This lack of certainty is really a good thing. If you take the flexibility out of a workplace, it becomes brittle and fragile. In any event, you cannot anticipate all issues and disputes that may arise in the time period following the creation or renewal of a framework and the collective agreement. The framework and the collective agreement should be viewed as organic — they are alive and subject to ongoing change. Complaints and disputes are inevitable about the application of the framework and the limitations imposed by the collective agreement. Employees and their union representatives are bound to think that they have a better way to do things, and maybe they do. An effective grievance and arbitration procedure acts as a problem-solving mechanism, which usually succeeds without the need for an arbitration hearing, and should lead to the calm, rational and open resolution of workplace discontent.

To return to a consistent theme, the front-line supervisor plays a key role in the early steps of the grievance procedure in terms of dealing with the initial complaint and, if necessary, the original recitation of the grievance. In the later stages, the process usually becomes more formal and the involvement of senior management and human resources becomes more prominent. Since the front-line supervisor usually has the best information about the circumstances of the complaint, s/he should remain involved throughout the process, even though the ultimate decision may be made at a higher level within the management team.

Nowhere is the front-line supervisor more important than at the initial oral complaint stage. In negotiating or reviewing the grievance procedure, do not take away the essential informality that should exist at the very beginning. The requirement that all complaints and suggestions be raised directly with the front-line supervisor in the normal course of day-to-day communications remains an integral first step in the grievance process. This step provides an opportunity for the supervisor and employee to resolve the problem quickly and with the least amount of fuss.

At this initial stage, neither a complaint nor the response is written. Since the intention is to have the complaint expressed orally and informally, do not expect a bright light to shine or a red arrow to appear over an employee's head to indicate that the complaint process has been initiated. The rule for a supervisor is that whenever an employee brings a suggestion or complaint to his or her attention, or questions an action, it is at least possible that the grievance procedure has been activated. The supervisor should respond, orally and promptly, in the required manner. The supervisor should make a brief note of any such situation, always following the W5 rule – who, what, why, when and where.

Front-line supervisors who have open communications with their workers may be able to get a tremendous amount of unfiltered information at the initial stage of a suggestion or complaint. If the situation passes on to more formal stages of the procedure, workers may get locked into positions that are no longer truly reflective of the original concern. Listen carefully at the outset and you may find a solution that, even if not originally accepted, can be resurrected at a later stage.

Responses and Resolutions to Complaints and Grievances

A front-line supervisor may have limited authority to resolve issues that are raised in suggestions and complaints, either at the initial oral stage or at the second stage, when a written grievance is filed. Even so, the supervisor should bear the primary responsibility for the initial investigation and the first responses, both orally and in writing. Naturally, the supervisor is part of the management team and should seek guidance and support in all but the most obvious cases from colleagues, superiors and the HRP.

If higher-level management becomes involved at later stages, they have to achieve a balance between trying to find a resolution that is satisfactory to everyone and trying to avoid contradicting or undercutting the authority of the front-line supervisor. Some of this balance can be achieved ahead of time by educating supervisors, especially if a worker has been subjected to corrective action. Supervisors have to understand that, while their decisions will be considered carefully and always respected, compromises may take place. Indeed, at the early stages of the procedure, supervisors may themselves be prepared to fashion compromises. At later stages, supervisors should be encouraged to participate in trying to find an effective compromise. It must be remembered by all members of the management team that for some cases, perhaps most cases, there is no acceptable compromise. You should always try to avoid compromising for the sake of compromise, as this simply may lead you into more complaints.

On the other hand, there are always some cases where compromise or even a complete retreat is appropriate. This may make sense for an individual case, but also for the entire system of complaints and grievances, if you want it to be effective. It is hard to have an effective procedure for suggestions and complaints from workers if the answer is always "no". Sometimes, "no" is the only appropriate answer, but not always. To determine what the answer should be in any particular situation, here are some guidelines:

1. Do not jump to conclusions. Wait until you have all the facts and circumstances behind the suggestion or complaint before responding.

2. Settle the issue on its merits. Provide the worker with his/her entitlement under the framework and the collective agreement. When the facts and circumstances fully support management's actions, say "no". On the other hand, admit mistakes graciously and promptly, and grant an appropriate remedy. Whatever you decide, provide a reasonable explanation of the reasons for your decision to the employee.

3. If your position is that the worker is not entitled to any remedy or benefit, or if you reject a suggestion, the written response should be fairly simple and straightforward. Depending on the nature of the issue, the response could reinforce the framework or confirm the appropriateness of a position classification, performance appraisal or corrective action.

4. The procedure for receiving complaints and filing grievances will almost certainly have time guidelines set out in the collective agreement. If the worker and his or her union representatives do not adhere to the guidelines, it may be appropriate to refuse to consider the complaint or suggestion. Management could be flexible in this respect, but you should always make clear to a worker when a complaint or grievance is untimely, so that you can make a preliminary objection at arbitration.

5. Carefully consider the implications of any settlement. Even if you ensure that it has no legal effect, this employee and other workers could still view it as an indication of how management will act in response to similar situations in the future. As a general rule, you should avoid "nuisance" settlements, as they only encourage

frivolous complaints. If senior management settles on this basis, often they are completely undercutting the supervisor, thereby turning a minor issue into a major problem within the management team. By "nuisance" settlement, I mean those situations where the worker or the union has no basis for a claim, but it is such a minor cost that you give in to what the worker or union has asked for.

6. If you are prepared to provide some benefit or remedy as a result of the complaint or grievance, you should get a written settlement, either as a separate document, or as a sign-back from the union on the grievance form. Here are important elements of any written settlement:

   • identify the complaint or grievance in question;
   • indicate that the parties have reached a settlement;
   • clearly state the terms of the settlement;
   • stipulate that the worker is satisfied that there has been a complete resolution;
   • in most cases, you should indicate that the settlement is without admission of liability, is without prejudice and does not constitute a precedent for other employees; this means that the settlement could not be introduced in a subsequent legal proceeding (in particular an arbitration) as evidence of the employer's view as to its legal position in this situation or a similar situation;
   • in some cases, you will want the settlement, or at least parts of it, to create a precedent, so be clear about your intention in that respect; and
   • in every case, carefully consider the implications and impact of a proposed settlement.

Proactive Steps to Avoid Unnecessary Complaints

As mentioned earlier, the front-line supervisor is responsible for attempting to detect and resolve problems at the earliest possible opportunity. A concerted effort to avoid unnecessary complaints should not compromise any of management's rights. In fact, listening to your employees and trying to resolve problems before they actually materialize into a formal grievance incorporates sound management principles and should enhance the effectiveness of the management team.

Here is a review of some important features in avoiding unnecessary complaints:

1. Communicate with your workers. Do not be reluctant to explain your actions or planned changes to your people.
2. If a worker tells you about a problem or complaint, ensure that s/he is kept informed of what you are doing about it. A worker will often be patient so long as s/he knows that the problem is being considered, not ignored.
3. Listen carefully and between the lines. If a problem seems trivial, try to understand what is the real basis for the complaint.
4. Act promptly to deal with the complaint, but avoid making snap judgments. Impulsive actions or statements often lead to mistakes. However, unjustified delay will likely frustrate the employee and could make a simple issue more serious and lead to an unnecessary, or unnecessarily contentious, grievance.
5. Avoid creating an atmosphere where employees feel that the only way to obtain consideration of their problems is through filing and pursuing a written grievance.
6. Treat each situation as unique. No two problems are completely identical and, therefore, identical solutions to problems that may seem to be similar may not be appropriate. Supervisors should get any necessary approvals before you indicate or promise anything to the employee.
7. Do not make commitments or promises that you cannot keep. Do not raise expectations that cannot be met.
8. Admit your mistakes and correct them as soon are you are aware that an error has been made. Covering up or trying to circumvent the framework will only damage your reputation with your employees and the union. Your employees' respect and trust in your integrity will increase when they realize that you readily admit mistakes but stand firm when you are right. Trust is important for union representatives as well. They may have to take adversarial positions, but it is much easier to work towards a resolution if they believe you and respect you.
9. Provide the employees with their entitlement under the framework and the collective agreement. Apply the framework and exercise your discretion under the collective agreement in a consistent, reasonable and unbiased manner.

◆
CHAPTER 8

RENEWAL AND CHANGE

C hange is inevitable. The old joke about life is that the one who has the most at the end wins. While some religions and philosophies suggest that there is a state of perfect balance that might be achievable in this lifetime, the next one, or one some other one, I am unaware of a state of perfect harmony for an organization. The only state of existence for an organization that seems certain is that it will be different tomorrow than it is today. Unlike the joke, the workplace is not a race to the end, it is an ongoing process.

You Never Actually Get There

On my fridge is a magnet with a saying that will be common to most of you, "life is a journey, not a destination". That is certainly true for most organizations. Unless they are set up for a limited purpose or for a limited period of time, most organizations have an indefinite existence. For most of us, life within our workplaces is an ongoing journey. We never actually arrive. The best that we can hope for, especially in terms of human resources management, is to get close to where we want to be. If you think you are where you want to be, you are likely delusional or entirely without ambition. I doubt that anybody who thinks that s/he is already there would be reading this book, or, if you started, you will not have bothered to get this far.

Whether we are far away, very close to where we want to be or, by miracle or illusion, finally there, it is not a fixed state. You will have to keep changing or change will keep happening to you. Your destination, assuming that you can define an ideal framework for human resources management with reasonable accuracy, is a moving target. If you ever get close, you will have to keep moving to stay close. Indeed, you will likely find that something that got you close, or at least moved you ahead at one point in the evolution of your organization, is no longer valid or helpful.

Everything I say about the inevitability of change is particularly true in unionized workplaces. Whatever your direction, and however much co-operation you may have with the union, you are not heading in the same direction. The union wants to get the best deal for its members. The employer wants to get the most it can from its workers.

Once you accept that constant evolution is innately human and as much a part of our organizations as it is of our individual selves, then you should have no problem adopting the notion that continuous renewal is not only necessary, it should be an integral part of your human resources framework. As noted, this is especially true in a unionized workplace. You should plan for change. You should lead change. Whatever is bad in your workplace can be made less so. Whatever is good can be made better. Whatever is excellent must be constantly nourished and reinforced. Indeed, you want to ride the crest of excellence in one area of your workplace to improve other areas that lag behind.

The Calendar System

Your framework will have key elements, depending on the nature of your workplace. Every framework should have safety and human rights as two of the elements; indeed, human rights could be further divided into discrimination (especially in terms of persons with disabilities) and harassment (especially sexual or racial harassment). Other key elements may include attendance, individual performance evaluation – featuring quality of production or service, and training in maintaining skills and acquiring new skills.

I suggest that you start with four or five key elements and stop at eight or nine. Assign a month to each of the elements. Avoid the month of your fiscal year end. Avoid December and avoid your two or three primary vacation months (typically the summer).

In each assigned month, every year, you will do the following:

- review and revise the relevant parts of the framework, including the collective agreement and any policies, procedures, rules or practices that might apply, as well as any materials that may have been produced, such as employee booklets or posted notices;
- in the course of your review, you should seek input from all employees and their union representatives, as discussed in section 5(d) above;
- communicate the key aspects of the element in question and conduct training, first of the management team and then of your workers and other employees; and

- complete any related tasks, such as performance evaluations in your quality month or a comprehensive safety inspection in safety month.

Paradigms for Learning

Whether you are the trainer or you are being trained yourself, it is important to focus on using the information to achieve a positive change in management practices. You should engage in training with a clear approach in mind for giving or receiving the information in a manner that will allow it to be put to practical use in the workplace.

There are two approaches to learning that you are encouraged to consider as an appropriate framework for the materials presented in this book. The first approach is called VISION; the second is called LEADER. Here is each one in summary form:

VISION	LEADER
√ Visualize	√ Leadership
√ Internalize	√ Excellence
√ Scrutinize	√ Action
√ Inform	√ Documentation
√ Organize	√ Evidence
√ Normalize – Now Go Do It!	√ Responsibility

The two approaches work together and should be viewed as two different angles on improving your human resources management and maintaining control of a unionized workplace. You may well come up with your own approaches. Indeed, it is a good exercise, as you read these materials, to try to develop your own personal framework that you can use afterwards to guide you in implementing effective workplace practices.

VISION

VISION is a collection of ideas that you should find applicable in any training situation, whether you are giving the training or receiving it, and whether the training consists of reading a book or listening to an oral presentation. The point of VISION is to access the materials in a direct and personal way. This may be a book that is written by Jamie Knight, but it is also a book that is read by each of you. As soon as you start reading my book, it becomes your book. Each of you will have a different experience with the book, depending on your own background, as well as the energy and intelligence that you put into reading the ideas contained in these pages. If the ideas in my book are to be effective in your workplace, then you have to transform my ideas into your ideas. In other words, VISION is not mine, it is meant to be yours.

- Visualize: As you read these materials, try to think about situations within your experience or imagination that relate to what you are reading. Translate the best of what is in these pages into training exercises; create case studies out of the concepts that you are learning about.

- Internalize: As you read and visualize situations to which you can relate, try to make your own sense of what you are reading. Make connections between the concepts in these pages and your own knowledge and experience. Whether or not you are experienced in human resources management, you likely have a significant set of skills that is unique and certainly valuable. These pages are not meant to create something out of nothing; rather they should challenge, shape and augment the knowledge that is already part of you.

- Scrutinize: There is no single source of all knowledge. You will not find all of the answers in one place. It is rare, if it ever happens, that you will read something or listen to something and accept all of it as right and good. Read critically. Make sure that what you are reading makes sense for you and your organization. Most importantly, if it does not make sense, do not be simply dismissive — that is too easy and lazy. Come up with your own better answer and connect it with other concepts that make better sense.

- **Inform:** Inform yourself and inform others. You should not read this book in one sitting. Indeed, you probably should not even read it from front to back. Treat it like a collective agreement. Scribble all over it. Highlight it. Underline it. Most importantly, discuss it, with your colleagues, with your superiors, and even with the people whom you supervise. Human resources management is not a solitary pursuit. Do not try to learn in isolation.

- **Organize:** As you visualize, internalize, scrutinize and inform yourself and others about these ideas and your own related ideas, organize all of this knowledge so that you can make sense of it and apply it. Patterns and systems for organization have been suggested throughout these materials, including VISION and LEADER. Feel free to create and use your own patterns and systems. Once you are done with this book, you should not be lost in a mess of new ideas. Rather, you should have a system, based in your prior knowledge and experience, which will allow you to manage people at your workplace even better than before.

- **Normalize:** With a system in place, you should be able to put some new ideas into action. Never try to do everything at once. Whole-scale changes in human resources management practices are generally counter-productive and even dangerous, especially in a unionized workplace. Remember that the union is conservative by nature and suspicious of significant and rapid change. Effective change is usually incremental, patiently implemented by management and made easy for the affected workplace players to digest.

    Pick two or three of the best ideas that come out of reading this book. Put those ideas into place in an organized and staged manner. Do not wait for a better idea to come along; as soon as you have a couple of good ideas, get to work. If the first changes are successful, and when you feel that your organization is ready for more change, pick the next two or three ideas and implement those. Not everything is going to work, but most should, especially if you are committed to the process of change.

    These changes are like plants — you cannot just pop the seed into the ground and hope for the best. You have to nurture the change and make it part of your normal workplace environment. Indeed, even when the change has firmly taken root, you have to revisit it from time to time to make sure that it is still healthy and not choked off by the weeds of ignorance and apathy.

LEADER

Although this book makes frequent reference to the *management* of human resources, it is also a key recommendation of the book that you should aspire to *leadership*. For our purposes, leadership is not meant to be a more highly developed form of management. The two act together. Leadership without management would be chaos. It would be like the meetings that too many of us attend where there are fantastic and creative ideas, but no action is ever taken.

Management without leadership is at best merely adequate and at worst without purpose. We all have to put out fires in our workplaces, often on a daily basis. If you spend all of your time putting out fires, then you are simply coping — you are not going anywhere. There is no point in being organized and efficient if you have no direction. It is for that reason that the word efficient should always be joined with the word effective — do it well, but do it with a clear objective in mind. Another coupling to remember is that it is important to be reactive (management), but you must also be proactive (leadership).

- Leadership: Do not simply manage. Learn from yesterday. Plan for tomorrow. Act today. This is your workplace. You are part of the brain of the employer. Where do you want to take the workplace today and in the years to come?

- Excellence: This is your workplace. You set the standards. Set your standards high. Excellence should be your goal, not just good enough.

- Action: Do something! Most mistakes in human resources management and in leading people happen because nothing was done when something should have been done. There are usually different things that could be done. Within reason, any one of those possibilities is probably better than doing nothing at all. If you keep sweeping everything under the rug, then eventually the rug is going to smell bad. If you keep running away from confrontation, then you will soon run away from your job as well.

- **D**ocumentation: Cover your assets — yours and the organization that employs you. You cannot remember everything. Make notes of any interesting situations that occur in your workplace and more structured reports when warranted. Use formal communication systems when you have something formal to communicate, like discipline or policies or standard operating procedures. Make life easier. Develop forms for the most common kinds of written communications. Follow a standard reporting system — W5: who, what, why, when and where. You should usually have recommendations to make; otherwise, keep your reports factual — leave your opinions out of them. With practice and a consistent system, you will find that you can make a decent initial note very quickly, often in a minute or two.

- **E**vidence: Preserve the present. If there are items that relate to a situation (a tool or scrap product perhaps), then you should consider hanging on to those items until the situation is fully resolved. Take photographs or videos. Use diagrams — even your own bad scratching will be much better than nothing at all. Use existing blueprints or schematics if relevant. Arbitration hearings may take place months after the event — you cannot create evidence just before the hearing, it has to be there all along.

- **R**esponsibility: Pass the buck if you do not have the full or final authority to take action in any particular situation. But always pass the buck with value added. You are not simply a messenger if you are part of the management team. You are part of the management brain. You are expected to contribute to decision making even if the final decision is not yours. Manage your own boss by giving your boss all of the information that he or she requires in order to make the decision that you think is best for the organization.

Continuous Improvement

Throughout the pages of this book, you have been encouraged to manage the situations that arise in your workplace in a manner that is efficient and that solves problems. You also have been challenged to look for opportunities to lead your workplace. You should feel empowered to seek out and be at the forefront of continuous improvement in your workplace. Continuous improvement in human resources management will make your workplace more efficient, more effective, more productive, and less subject to undue influence by the union. Your job is to operate the workplace in a way that makes sense to the objectives of the employer and not to be pushed off course by union demands or expectations that are inconsistent with those objectives.

Continuous improvement is not simply a catchy concept; it should be an objective at the heart of any organization. Whatever you are doing today, and however well you are doing it, you could be doing it better tomorrow. To do it better, you may have to make significant changes. Effective and long-lasting change takes time to implement, so you had better get busy with changes that make sense for your workplace, and stay busy throughout your career.

Index

introducing problem at meeting, 112
ways in which employment contract terminated, 22-23
  business failure, 22
  cause, for, 22
  constructive dismissal, 22
  frustration of contract, 22
  reasonable notice, 23
  resignation or retirement, 23
wrongful dismissal, 19-20, 23

Framework, creating
buy-in with management team and workers, creating, 69-71
  generally, 69-70
  implementing suggestions, seeking out opportunities for, 70-71
  promoting understanding of framework, 71
    after achievement of collective agreement, 71
  widespread input before finalizing framework, 70
generally, 53-54
  common law and legal requirements, absorbing, 53
input while maintaining control, gaining, 72-73
  HRP overseeing process and setting timeframe, 72
  HRP managing input process, 72-73
    tactics suggested, 72-73
  participation, fostering meaningful, 73
  union input, seeking, 72
introduction, 61-62
  comparison with other organizations, 61-62
  self-audit, 61
new or improved framework, creating, 66-69
  co-ordinated and cohesive set of materials, achieving, 68-69
    your tidy desk, 68
  grouping of employees, 66
    bargaining units, 66
    sub-groups, 66
  policies, establishing or reviewing and revising, 66
  procedures relating to human rights, health and safety,
    job evaluation, postings and scheduling, 67-68
  procedures relating to warnings and employee complaints
    establishing or reviewing and revising, 67
  specific rules, establishing or reviewing and revising, 68

open communications, importance of, 126
responses and resolutions to complaints and grievances,
126-127, 130
issues for grievances, 124-126
improper classification of worker, 124
improper interpretation of collective agreement, 124
management rights vs. collective agreement, 124-125
unjust discipline, 124
organic framework, 125
problem-solving mechanism, 125
pyramid depiction, 117
responses and resolutions to complaints and grievances, 126-128
front-line supervisor's responsibility, 126-127, 130
supervisor bearing primary responsibility for first responses,
126, 130
supervisor encouraged to participate in finding compromise,
126-127
guidelines in deciding whether to compromise, 127-128
implications of settlement, careful consideration of, 128
"nuisance" settlements, 128
settling issue on its merits, 127
time guidelines, adhering to, 127
waiting for all facts and circumstances, 127
written response, simple and straightforward, 127
written settlement, 128
higher-level management involvement, 126
balance, achieving, 126
settlement, advantages of, 113-114
settlement, written, 128
important elements, 128
unnecessary complaints, 129-130
proactive steps to avoid, 129-130
review of important features in avoiding, 129-130

Human rights
discrimination, prohibition against, 41
barriers to effective recruitment, hiring and promotion practices,
41-42
bad for business or illegal, 42
harassment, prohibition against, 41, 42

Renewal and change
calendar system, 59, 132-133
   key elements of human resources policy, 59, 132
   reviewing and revising parts of framework, 59, 132
   steps in each assigned month, 132-133
constant evolution, 132
continuous improvement, 137-138
dealing with unexpected, 58-59
generally, 131
learning paradigms, 133-137
   LEADER approach, 133, 136-137
     action, 136
     documentation, 137
     evidence, 137
     excellence, 136
     generally, 136
     leadership, 136
     responsibility, 137
   VISION approach, 133-136
     best ideas, implementing and nurturing, 135-136
     generally, 133-134
     inform, 135
     internalize, 134
     normalize, 135
     organize, 135
     scrutinize, 134
     visualize, 134
managing change, 59, 131-132
responding to change, 58
unionized workplace, change inevitable in, 131-132

Statutory law *See* **Boundaries of human resources management**

Suggestion and complaint procedure
arbitration, 121-124
   argument, 124
     jurisprudence, 124
     "PING-PONG-ping" sequence, 124
   burden of proof, 121